COOKBOOK TO LOWER CHOLESTEROL

200+ FLAVORFUL AND EASY RECIPES FOR A HEALTHY HEART
AND LOWER CHOLESTEROL NATURALLY.
TASTY MEALS TO REDUCE BAD FAT

Audrey Harris

This book includes free bonus recipes that are available here:

You can also Join the People Writers Special Newsletter
and be the first to find out about our new books!
You can find our catalog at Peoplewriters.com
And all books for sale on Amazon.com

SPECIAL REQUEST – GIVE US A REVIEW!
Your review can help us a lot.
If you liked this book, go to Amazon.com
and leave a review!

© Copyright 2022 - All rights reserved.

The content contained within this book may not be reproduced, duplicated or transmitted without direct written permission from the author or the publisher.

Under no circumstances will any blame or legal responsibility be held against the publisher, or author, for any damages, reparation, or monetary loss due to the information contained within this book. Either directly or indirectly.

Legal Notice:

This book is copyright protected. This book is only for personal use. You cannot amend, distribute, sell, use, quote or paraphrase any part, or the content within this book, without the consent of the author or publisher.

Disclaimer Notice:

Please note the information contained within this document is for educational and entertainment purposes only. All effort has been executed to present accurate, up to date, and reliable, complete information. No warranties of any kind are declared or implied. Readers acknowledge that the author is not engaging in the rendering of legal, financial, medical or professional advice. The content within this book has been derived from various sources. Please consult a licensed professional before attempting any techniques outlined in this book.

By reading this document, the reader agrees that under no circumstances is the author responsible for any losses, direct or indirect, which are incurred as a result of the use of information contained within this document, including, but not limited to, — errors, omissions, or inaccuracies.

TABLE OF CONTENTS

INTRODUCTION 13

BREAKFAST 14
1. Fruity Mango Creamy Chia Pudding 15
2. Crispy Chickpea Omelet With Garlic 16
3. Smooth Cashew Cream and Fruit Parfait 17
4. Cinnamon Raisin Quinoa Breakfast Porridge 18
5. Banana Bread Breakfast With Magical Sunflower Seed 19
6. Breakfast Quesadilla 20
7. Hummus and Date Bagel 20
8. Curry Tofu Scramble 21
9. Breakfast Splits 21
10. Tomato Basil Bruschetta 22
11. Cucumber Avocado Toast With Sesame Seeds 23
12. Yams and Cabbage Hash With Sage 24
13. Overnight Berry Chia Oats 25
14. Raspberry Vanilla Smoothie 25
15. Blueberry Banana Protein Smoothie 26
16. Chocolate Banana Smoothie 26
17. Moroccan Avocado Smoothie 27
18. Greek Yogurt With Fresh Berries, Honey, and Nuts 27
19. Mediterranean Egg Muffins With Ham 28
20. Quinoa Bake With Banana 29
21. Sun-Dried Tomatoes, Dill, and Feta Omelet Casserole 30
22. Breakfast Taco Scramble 31
23. Green Protein Papaya Smoothie 32
24. Oatmeal With Fruit and Nuts 33
25. Magic of Vegetable Pancakes 34
26. Brunch-Style Portobello Mushrooms 35
27. Pear-Blueberry Granola 36
28. Bagel Avocado Toast 37
29. Tropical Yogurt 37
30. Smoked Salmon Breakfast Wraps 38

31. Mixed-Grain Muesli 39
32. Breakfast Parfaits 40
33. Blueberry Muffins 41
34. Cinnamon Streusel Rolls 42
35. Apple Cinnamon Chia Pudding 43
36. Watermelon and Berry Salad With Buckwheat 44
37. Healthy Breakfast Muffins 45
38. Turkey Breakfast Sausage 46
39. Vegetable Omelet 47
40. Breakfast Potatoes 48
41. Couscous Cereal With Fruit 48
42. French Toast 49
43. Pasta Frittata 50
44. Overnight Cherry-Almond Oatmeal 51
45. Banana Oatmeal Pancakes 51
46. Garlic-Herb Mini Quiches 52
47. Yogurt and Honey Fruit Cups 52
48. Oatmeal Waffles 53
49. Chicken and Asparagus Crepes 54
50. Banana Oat Breakfast Cookies 55

LUNCH 56
51. Coconut and Peanut Aubergine Curry 57
52. Orange Bell Peppers Curry 58
53. Roasted Broccoli With Lemon 59
54. Tofu and Kale Sandwich 60
55. Sesame-Ginger Marinated Vegetables 61
56. Tofu and Vegetable Curry 62
57. Pad Thai 63
58. Strip Steak Quinoa 64
59. Delightful Stuffed Lamb With Peppers 65
60. Chopped Lambs With Rosemary 66
61. Baked Mackerel With Artichokes and Almonds 67

62. Baked Tuna Fillets on Cream of Carrots and Pistachios 68
63. Chickpea Soup 69
64. Lentil Salad From Heaven With Baby Spinach 70
65. Tomato, Chickpea, and Sweet Potato Soup 71
66. Butterbeans Kale Salad 72
67. Beans and Millet Salad With Spinach and Lemon 73
68. Butternut Squash and Quinoa Mason Jar Salad 74
69. Spicy Lime Pork Tenderloins 75
70. Garlic Turkey Skewers 75
71. Almond Butter Chicken 76
72. Balsamic Berry Chicken 77
73. Spicy Trout Sheet Pan Dinner 78
74. Maple-Garlic Salmon and Cauliflower Sheet Pan Dinner 79
75. Salmon Patties 80
76. Sweet Salad Dressing Chicken and Carrot Sheet Pan Dinner 81
77. Chicken, Mushroom, and Bell Pepper Skewers 82
78. Chicken Curry 83
79. Lemon Chicken and Asparagus 84
80. Turkey Quinoa Casserole 85
81. Sheet Pan Honey-Soy Beef Broccoli 86
82. Heart-Healthy Meatloaf 87
83. Easy Lean Beef With Carrots and Potatoes 88
84. Spicy Honey Chicken and Eggplant 89
85. Turkey Meatballs 90
86. Greek Pizza 91
87. Spinach, Walnut, and Black Bean Burgers 92
88. Loaded Veggie-Stuffed Peppers 93
89. Chicken With Black Olives, Capers, and Rice Oil 94
90. Basil Pesto Chicken 95
91. Olive Turkey Patties 96
92. Broccoli Chicken Rice 97
93. Chicken Meatballs 98
94. Parmesan Pork Chops 99

95. Cannellini Bean Lettuce Wraps 100
96. Israeli Eggplant, Chickpea, and Mint Sauté 101
97. Minestrone Chickpeas and Macaroni Casserole 102
98. Spiced Soup With Lentils and Legumes 103
99. Brown Rice Pilaf With Golden Raisins 104
100. Ritzy Veggie Chili 105

DINNER 106
101. Roasted Shrimp and Veggies 107
102. Shrimp and Pineapple Lettuce Wraps 108
103. Grilled Scallops With Gremolata 109
104. Healthy Paella 110
105. Vietnamese Fish and Noodle Bowl 111
106. Cod Satay 112
107. Crispy Mixed Nut Fish Fillets 113
108. Steamed Sole Rolls With Greens 114
109. Red Snapper Scampi 115
110. Green Rice Salad With Tomatoes 116
111. Orange Thyme Red Snapper 117
112. Farro Veggie Pilaf 118
113. Buckwheat Veggie Pilaf 119
114. Amaranth With Artichokes and Garlic 120
115. Fruited Quinoa Salad 121
116. Warm Teff Chutney Salad 122
117. Teff With Broccoli Pesto 123
118. Warm Barley Salad With Spring Veggies 124
119. Smashed Baby Potatoes 125
120. Skillet-Roasted Sweet Potatoes 126
121. Mashed Sweet Potatoes With Nut and Seed Topping 127
122. Grilled Sweet Potatoes and Peppers 128
123. One-Pot Veggie Pasta 129
124. Pasta Puttanesca 130
125. Vegetable Egg Fried Rice 131

126. Tuna in Potatoes 132
127. Shrimp Scampi 133
128. Shrimp Boil 134
129. Shrimp and Sausage Gumbo 135
130. Fish Stew 136
131. Salmon With Lemon and Dill 137
132. Duck and Blackberries 138
133. Ginger Duck Mix 139
134. Asparagus Smoked Salmon 140
135. Salmon With Caper Sauce 141
136. Vietnamese Braised Catfish 142
137. Duck, Cucumber, and Mango Salad 143
138. Duck and Orange Warm Salad 144
139. Creamy Coriander Chicken 145
140. Lemony Turkey and Pine Nuts 146
141. Creamy Chicken and Mushrooms 147
142. Oregano Turkey and Peppers 148
143. Turkey and Cranberry Sauce 149
144. Chicken and Mint Sauce 149
145. Curry Chicken, Artichokes, and Olives 150
146. Chili Prawns 151
147. Tuna Salpicao 152
148. Soy-Ginger Braised Squid 153
149. Sea Bass in Coconut Cream Sauce 154
150. Cod Chowder 155

DESSERT 156
151. Dessert Pizza 157
152. Lemon Biscotti 158
153. Rice Pudding With Dried Figs 159
154. Greek Parfait With Mixed Berries 160
155. Fruit Kabobs With Yogurt Deep 160
156. No-Bake Chocolate Squares 161

157. Stuffed Dried Figs 161
158. Feta Cheesecake 162
159. Greek-Style Chocolate Semifreddo 163
160. Traditional Italian Cake With Almonds 164
161. Pear Croustade 165
162. Kourabiedes Almond Cookies 166
163. Revani Syrup Cake 167
164. Almonds and Oats Pudding 168
165. Mediterranean Tomato Salad With Feta and Fresh Herbs 169
166. Quinoa Bowl With Yogurt, Dates, and Almonds 170
167. Almond Butter Banana Chocolate Smoothie 171
168. Loukoumades (Fried Honey Balls) 172
169. Crème Caramel 173
170. Fruitcake 174
171. Fruited Rice Pudding 175
172. Sauteed Bananas 176
173. Banana Mousse 177
174. Wacky Chocolate Cake 178
175. Vanilla Poached Peaches 179
176. Berry Cobbler 180
177. Carrot and Spice Quick Bread 181
178. Grapes and Lemon Sour Cream Sauce 182
179. Orange Dream Smoothie 183
180. Rustic Apple-Cranberry Tart 184
181. Strawberries and Cream 185
182. Whole-Grain Banana Bread 186
183. Honey Grilled Apples 187
184. Apple Tapioca 187
185. Sweet Potato Pudding 188
186. Pumpkin Cookies 189
187. Mascarpone and Fig Crostini 190
188. Traditional Mediterranean Lokum 191
189. Mixed Berry and Fig Compote 192

190. Creamed Fruit Salad 192
191. Almond Cookies 193
192. Crunchy Sesame Cookies 194
193. Mini Orange Tarts 195
194. Traditional Kalo Prama 196
195. Turkish-Style Chocolate Halva 197
196. Cookies and Cream Shake 198
197. Lemon Cheesecake 198
198. Whole-Grain Mixed Berry Coffeecake 199
199. Almond and Apricot Biscotti 200
200. Apple Dumplings 201

CONCLUSION 203

INTRODUCTION

Why is healthy living becoming more popular with each passing day? More and more people are becoming interested in developing their own lifestyle that is not just limited to the practice of regular exercise but also includes healthy food choices. The problem with this new trend towards healthier living is the difficulty in finding information. When beginning a new lifestyle change, one of the first things most people do is check online for examples of potential modifications to their diet. When consumers want to make a change, for example, they need to be well-informed so that they can take ownership of their health.

If you are trying to lower your cholesterol, the first thing you need to do is educate yourself on this health problem so you can take control of your situation. All too often people blame their lack of success in lowering their cholesterol on someone else or something beyond their control. This is not a healthy way to think and it can lead to frustration and anger as well as depression over having to change your habits or lifestyle.

Instead, think about it from another angle with the understanding that all situations in life involve change—whether we choose them or not. People need to be prepared for those changes rather than being caught off guard by them.

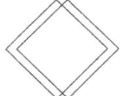

BREAKFAST

1. FRUITY MANGO CREAMY CHIA PUDDING

Preparation Time
10 minutes

Cooking Time
10 minutes

Servings
2

INGREDIENTS

- ¼ lb frozen mango chunks
- 1 (6 oz) can of lite coconut milk
- 3 tbsp chia seeds
- 1 drop of almond extract
- Juice of ½ lime
- ½ cup sugar

DIRECTIONS

1. Put the chia seeds in a bowl and add the coconut milk with a drop of almond extract.
2. Stir with a spoon until well-mixed. Cover the bowl and leave it to soak for at least 2 hours or even overnight. Remember, the coconut milk will thicken until it solidifies and will need to be heated up to thin it again.
3. Place the mango chunks in a blender saving a few chunks for later. Add the lime juice to the blender and mix until smooth and thick.
4. To prepare your pudding: Put a few spoons of mango puree into a glass and follow with a layer of the chia mixture. Repeat the process with all the mixture.
5. Put a piece of mango on top of your pudding and serve.

Nutritions: Calories: 228.8; Total fat: 6.9 g; Saturated fat: 0.4 g; Polyunsaturated fat: 2.7 g; Monounsaturated fat: 1.8 g; Cholesterol: 0.0 mg; Sodium: 34.8 mg; Potassium: 501.3 mg; Total carbohydrates: 30.8 g; Dietary fiber: 16.6 g; Sugar: 6.8 g; Protein: 11.9 g

2. CRISPY CHICKPEA OMELET WITH GARLIC

Preparation Time
10 minutes

Cooking Time
5 minutes

Servings
4

INGREDIENTS

- 1 cup chickpea flour
- ½ cup + 2 tbsp unsweetened non-dairy milk
- 4 tsp apple cider vinegar
- 4 tsp nutritional yeast (optional)
- ½ tsp turmeric powder
- ½ tsp garlic powder
- ½ tsp onion powder
- ½ tsp baking soda
- ½ tsp sea salt to taste

For the stuffing options:
- ½ red onion, chopped
- 4 garlic cloves, minced
- ½ cup tomatoes, chopped
- ½ cup small broccoli florets
- 2 tbsp coriander

DIRECTIONS

1. In a Pyrex measuring cup, mix the chickpea ingredients. Do not make the mix too thick to stir. It should be like pancake batter, easy to pour. Allow it to sit.
2. Fry the red onion and garlic in a hot coated pan until lightly browned. Add the broccoli to soften. Remove and place on a plate.
3. Put some olive oil into the pan and add half of the mixture to it. Add garlic, onion, broccoli, and tomatoes, and wait for it to bubble.
4. Turn over to cook for a minute. Cover with a lid, turn off the heat, and leave for 5 minutes.
5. Garnish with tomatoes, chopped red onion, sliced avocado, and lime.
6. Add sea salt and pepper to taste.

Nutritions: Calories: 89.0; Total fat: 1.5 g; Saturated fat: 0.3 g; Polyunsaturated fat: 0.0 g; Monounsaturated fat: 0.0 g; Cholesterol: 0.0 mg; Sodium: 14.8 mg; Potassium: 0.0 mg; Total carbohydrates: 13.3 g; Dietary fiber: 2.5 g; Sugar: 2.5 g; Protein: 5.3 g

3. SMOOTH CASHEW CREAM AND FRUIT PARFAIT

Preparation Time
15 minutes

Cooking Time
15 minutes

Servings
4

INGREDIENTS

For the parfait:
- 3 cup soaked cashews
- 4 tbsp water
- 1 tsp orange zest
- 1/cup coconut oil
- ½ cup quinoa mixed with oats
- Juice of 2 oranges
- 6 tbsp maple syrup
- 2 tsp vanilla extract

DIRECTIONS

1. Blend all the ingredients together. The mixture has to be nice and thick, but if you're having trouble blending it, add 1 spoonful of extra water. Keep on one side for later.
2. Preheat the oven to 450°F.
3. Melt the coconut oil in the microwave and set aside.
4. Add the coconut oil and maple syrup and mix.
5. Pour the quinoa mix onto a baking sheet and use a spatula spread thinly. Bake for 15 minutes or until the edges are slightly darkened.
6. Remove from the oven and reserve.
7. Assemble: Add 1 spoonful of oatmeal to the bottom of each jar. Add the cashew cream and crunchy quinoa. Cover it with perfect pomegranate seeds.

Nutritions: Calories: 332; Total fat: 15.44 g; Saturated fat: 9.563 g; Polyunsaturated fat: 0.561 g; Monounsaturated fat: 4.342 g; Cholesterol: 58 mg; Sodium: 76 mg; Potassium: 190 mg; Total carbohydrates: 48.12 g; Dietary fiber: 0.9 g; Sugar: 27.85 g; Protein: 3.14 g

4. CINNAMON RAISIN QUINOA BREAKFAST PORRIDGE

Preparation Time
10 minutes

Cooking Time
2 minutes

Servings
2

INGREDIENTS

For the porridge:
- 1 ½ cup cooked quinoa
- ⅛ cup plain, unsweetened coconut milk
- 2 tbsp coconut sugar
- 1 tsp golden flaxseed meal
- 1 tsp raisins
- ⅜ tsp ground cinnamon
- 1 pinch salt
- ⅜ tsp pure vanilla extract

Topping ideas:
- Pomegranate seeds
- Chopped nuts
- Shredded coconut
- Chia seeds
- Cacao nibs

DIRECTIONS

1. Combine quinoa, coconut milk, sugar, flaxseed, raisins, cinnamon, and salt in a saucepan.
2. Bring to a boil over medium heat, then reduce the heat slightly and cook for 2-3 minutes with stirring vigorously. Turn off the heat and add the vanilla extract.
3. Serve hot with the toppings of your choice.

Nutritions: Calories: 136.0; Total fat: 1.0 g; Saturated fat: 0.2 g; Polyunsaturated fat: 0.4 g; Monounsaturated fat: 0.2 g; Cholesterol: 0.0 mg; Sodium: 2.5 mg; Potassium: 172.1 mg; Total carbohydrates: 28.5 g; Dietary fiber: 2.0 g; Sugar: 6.8 g; Protein: 3.1 g

5. BANANA BREAD BREAKFAST WITH MAGICAL SUNFLOWER SEED

Preparation Time
5 minutes

Cooking Time
5 minutes

Servings
2

INGREDIENTS

- 1 small frozen banana
- 3 tbsp oat flour
- 3 tbsp grounded sunflower seed
- ½ tsp baking powder
- ¼ tsp baking soda
- 3 tsp juice of your choice (like orange or apple juice)
- 1 tbsp sugar
- 1 cup berries of your choice

DIRECTIONS

1. Squash the banana in a small dish then add all the other ingredients. Blend well to make a soft and thick dough.
2. Spoon the dough into a microwavable muffin tray.
3. Microwave on high for 1–2 minutes. When cooked, the top should feel firm but soft. Remove from tray and put on cooling racks.

Nutritions: Calories: 84.2; Total fat: 0.2 g; Saturated fat: 0.0 g; Polyunsaturated fat: 0.1 g; Monounsaturated fat: 0.0 g; Cholesterol: 0.0 mg; Sodium: 96.2 mg; Potassium: 72.7 mg; Total carbohydrates: 19.5 g; Dietary fiber: 0.7 g; Sugar: 8.3 g; Protein: 1.6 g

6. BREAKFAST QUESADILLA

Preparation Time
5 minutes

Cooking Time
10 minutes

Servings
4

INGREDIENTS

- 1 cup egg substitute
- ¼ cup salsa
- ¼ cup low-fat Cheddar cheese, shredded
- 8 corn tortillas
- Nonstick olive oil spray

DIRECTIONS

1. Prepare the scrambled eggs using the egg substitute, and when almost ready, mix in the salsa and cheese.
2. Using a nonstick olive oil spray, lightly coat one side of the tortillas and arrange 4 of them oiled side down on a baking sheet.
3. Spread the egg mixture among the tortillas, smoothing it evenly. The remaining tortillas, oiled side up, go on top. Grill the quesadillas for 3 minutes on each side, or until golden brown. To serve, cut into quarters.

Nutritions: Calories: 152; Protein: 12 g; Carbohydrates: 18 g; Fat: 4 g; Cholesterol: 2 mg; Fiber: 3 g

7. HUMMUS AND DATE BAGEL

Preparation Time
3 minutes

Cooking Time
5 minutes

Servings
1

INGREDIENTS

- ¼ serving of homemade hummus or store-bought hummus
- 6 dates, pitted and halved
- 1 bagel
- Dash of salt and pepper
- 1 squeeze of lemon juice

DIRECTIONS

1. Split the bagel in half. In a toaster or under the broiler, toast the bagel.
2. Rub each side with hummus.
3. Add salt, dates, lemon juice and pepper to taste.

Nutritions: Calories: 410; Protein: 91 g; Carbohydrates: 59 g; Fat: 2 g; Cholesterol: 0 mg; Fiber: 9.7 g

8. CURRY TOFU SCRAMBLE

Preparation Time
5 minutes

Cooking Time
5 minutes

Servings
3

INGREDIENTS

- 1 tsp curry powder
- 1 tsp olive oil
- 12 oz crumbled tofu
- ¼ cup skim milk
- ¼ tsp chili flakes

DIRECTIONS

1. In a skillet, heat the olive oil. Toss in the tofu crumbles and chili flakes. Combine skim milk and curry powder in a mixing dish.
2. Stir thoroughly after pouring the liquid over crumbled tofu. On medium-high heat, scramble the tofu for 3 minutes.

Nutritions: Calories: 102; Protein: 10 g; Carbohydrates: 3.3 g; Fat: 6.4 g; Cholesterol: 0 mg; Fiber: 3 g

9. BREAKFAST SPLITS

Preparation Time
10 minutes

Cooking Time
0 minutes

Servings
2

INGREDIENTS

- 2 tbsp low-fat yogurt
- 2 peeled bananas
- 4 tbsp granola
- 1 chopped strawberry
- ½ tsp ground cinnamon

DIRECTIONS

1. Combine yogurt, ground cinnamon, and strawberries in a mixing dish.
2. Then cut the bananas lengthwise and fill them with the yogurt mass.
3. Granola may be sprinkled on top of the fruits.

Nutritions: Calories: 154; Protein: 6.8 g; Carbohydrates: 45.2 g; Fat: 8 g; Cholesterol: 1 mg; Fiber: 4 g

10. TOMATO BASIL BRUSCHETTA

Preparation Time
5 minutes

Cooking Time
10 minutes

Servings
6

INGREDIENTS	DIRECTIONS

- 2 tbsp chopped basil
- ½ whole-grain baguette, 6 ½-inch-thick diagonal slices
- 1 tbsp chopped parsley
- 3 diced tomatoes
- 2 minced garlic cloves
- 1 tsp olive oil
- ½ cup diced fennel
- 1 tsp black pepper
- 2 tsp balsamic vinegar

1. Preheat the oven to 400°F. The baguette pieces should be gently toasted. Combine all the remaining ingredients in a large mixing bowl.
2. Distribute the mixture equally over the toasted bread. Serve right away.

Nutritions: Calories: 142; Protein: 5 g; Carbohydrates: 26 g; Fat: 2 g; Cholesterol: 0 mg; Fiber: 2 g

11. CUCUMBER AVOCADO TOAST WITH SESAME SEEDS

Preparation Time
5 minutes

Cooking Time
0 minutes

Servings
2

INGREDIENTS

- 4 tbsp mashed avocado
- 2 slice sourdough bread, toasted
- 4 slices cucumber
- ½ tsp sesame seeds
- Salt to taste

DIRECTIONS

1. Spread the avocado on the toast.
2. Garnish with cucumber and sprinkle with sesame seeds and salt.

Nutritions: Calories: 380.9; Total fat: 21.0 g; Saturated fat: 3.1 g; Polyunsaturated fat: 4.9 g; Monounsaturated fat: 10.8 g; Cholesterol: 3.8 mg; Sodium: 431.3 mg; Potassium: 772.5 mg; Total carbohydrates: 44.9 g; Dietary fiber: 11.0 g; Sugar: 6.7 g; Protein: 9.0 g

12. YAMS AND CABBAGE HASH WITH SAGE

Preparation Time
5 minutes

Cooking Time
10 minutes

Servings
4

INGREDIENTS

- ½ medium yam
- 1 tsp olive oil
- 1 cup trimmed cabbage, halved
- ¼ cup onion
- 1/2 tsp oregano
- ¼ tsp sage
- ½ tbsp fresh chervil

DIRECTIONS

1. Preheat the oven to 390°F.
2. Peel and dice yams and cook them in a small saucepan for 2-3 minutes until they become soft (check with a fork).
3. In the meantime, heat a cast iron skillet over high heat, drizzle with olive oil and fry the cabbage and onions.
4. Drain the yams and put them into a pan with oregano, sage, and chervil.
5. Continue cooking for another 3 minutes stirring the vegetables and the herbs. Then pull it out from the oven.

Nutritions: Calories: 177.7; Total fat: 7.1 g; Saturated fat: 1.0 g; Polyunsaturated fat: 0.8 g; Monounsaturated fat: 5.0 g; Cholesterol: 0.0 mg; Sodium: 53.1 mg; Potassium: 745.3 mg; Total carbohydrates: 26.4 g; Dietary fiber: 6.0 g; Sugar: 9.7 g; Protein: 4.5 g

13. OVERNIGHT BERRY CHIA OATS

Preparation Time
15 minutes

Cooking Time
5 minutes

Servings
1

INGREDIENTS

- ½ cup Quaker Oats rolled oats
- ¼ cup chia seeds
- 1 cup milk or water
- A pinch of salt and cinnamon
- Maple syrup to taste (or a different sweetener)
- 1 cup frozen berries of your choice or smoothie leftovers

Toppings:
- Yogurt
- Berries

DIRECTIONS

1. In a jar with a lid, add the oats, seeds, milk, salt, and cinnamon and refrigerate overnight. On serving day, puree the berries in a blender.
2. Stir the oats, add in the berry puree, and top with yogurt and more berries, nuts, honey, or garnish of your choice. Enjoy!

Nutritions: Calories: 405; Carbs: 65 g; Fat: 11 g; Protein: 17 g

14. RASPBERRY VANILLA SMOOTHIE

Preparation Time
5 minutes

Cooking Time
5 minutes

Servings
2 cup

INGREDIENTS

- 1 cup frozen raspberries
- 1 (6 oz) container of vanilla Greek yogurt
- ½ cup unsweetened vanilla almond milk

DIRECTIONS

1. Take all of your ingredients and place them in a blender.
2. Process until smooth and liquified.

Nutritions: Calories: 155; Protein: 7 g; Fat: 2 g; Carbohydrates: 30 g

15. BLUEBERRY BANANA PROTEIN SMOOTHIE

Preparation Time
5 minutes

Cooking Time
5 minutes

Servings
1

INGREDIENTS

- ½ cup frozen and unsweetened blueberries
- ½ banana, sliced up
- ¾ cup plain nonfat Greek yogurt
- ¾ cup unsweetened vanilla almond milk
- 2 cup ice cubes

DIRECTIONS

1. Add all the ingredients to a blender. Blend until smooth.

Nutritions: Calories: 230; Protein: 19.1 g; Fat: 2.6 g; Carbohydrates: 32.9 g

16. CHOCOLATE BANANA SMOOTHIE

Preparation Time
5 minutes

Cooking Time
0 minutes

Servings
2

INGREDIENTS

- 2 bananas, peeled
- 1 cup unsweetened almond milk, or skim milk
- 1 cup crushed ice
- 3 tbsp unsweetened cocoa powder
- 3 tbsp honey

DIRECTIONS

1. In a blender, combine the bananas, almond milk, ice, cocoa powder, and honey.
2. Blend until smooth.

Nutritions: Calories: 219; Protein: 2 g; Carbohydrates: 57 g; Fat: 2 g

17. MOROCCAN AVOCADO SMOOTHIE

Preparation Time
5 minutes

Cooking Time
0 minutes

Servings
4

INGREDIENTS

- 1 ripe avocado, peeled and pitted
- 1 overripe banana
- 1 cup almond milk, unsweetened
- 1 cup ice

DIRECTIONS

1. Place the avocado, banana, milk, and ice into your blender.
2. Blend until smooth with no pieces of avocado remaining.

Nutritions: Calories: 100; Protein: 1 g; Fat: 6 g; Carbohydrates: 11 g

18. GREEK YOGURT WITH FRESH BERRIES, HONEY, AND NUTS

Preparation Time
5 minutes

Cooking Time
0 minutes

Servings
1

INGREDIENTS

- 6 oz non-fat plain Greek yogurt
- ½ cup fresh berries of your choice
- 1 tbsp crushed walnuts
- 1 tbsp honey

DIRECTIONS

1. In a jar with a lid, add the yogurt.
2. Top with berries, nuts, and a drizzle of honey.
3. Top with the lid and store in the fridge for 2-3 days.

Nutritions: Calories: 250; Carbs: 35 g; Fat: 4 g; Protein: 19 g

19. MEDITERRANEAN EGG MUFFINS WITH HAM

Preparation Time
15 minutes

Cooking Time
15 minutes

Servings
6

INGREDIENTS

- 9 slices of thin-cut deli ham
- ½ cup canned roasted red pepper, sliced + additional for garnish
- ⅓ cup fresh spinach, minced
- ¼ cup Feta cheese, crumbled
- 5 large eggs
- A pinch of salt
- A pinch of pepper
- 1 ½ tbsp Pesto sauce
- Fresh basil for garnish
- Cooking spray

DIRECTIONS

1. Preheat the oven to 400°F. Spray a muffin tin with cooking spray, generously. Line each of the muffin tins with 1 ½ piece of ham—making sure there aren't any holes for the egg mixture to come out.
2. Place some of the roasted red pepper in the bottom of each muffin tin. Place 1 tbsp minced spinach on top of each red pepper. Top the pepper and spinach off with a large ½ tbsp crumbled Feta cheese.
3. In a medium bowl, whisk together the eggs, salt, and pepper, and divide the egg mixture evenly among the 6 muffin tins.
4. Bake for 15-17 minutes until the eggs are puffy and set. Remove each cup from the muffin tin. Allow them to cool completely
5. Distribute the muffins among the containers and store them in the fridge for 2-3 days or in the freezer for 3 months.

Nutritions: Calories: 109; Carbs: 2 g; Fat: 6 g; Protein: 9 g

20. QUINOA BAKE WITH BANANA

Preparation Time
15 minutes

Cooking Time
1 hour and 10 minutes

Servings
8

INGREDIENTS

- 3 cup medium overripe bananas, mashed
- ¼ cup molasses
- ¼ cup pure maple syrup
- 1 tbsp cinnamon
- 2 tsp raw vanilla extract
- 1 tsp ground ginger
- 1 tsp ground cloves
- ½ tsp ground allspice
- ½ tsp salt
- 1 cup quinoa, uncooked
- 2 ½ cup unsweetened vanilla almond milk
- ¼ cup slivered almonds

DIRECTIONS

1. In the bottom of a 2.5-3-quart casserole dish, mix together the mashed banana, maple syrup, cinnamon, vanilla extract, ginger, cloves, allspice, molasses, and salt until well mixed.
2. Add in the quinoa and stir until the quinoa is evenly in the banana mixture. Whisk in the almond milk, mix until well combined, and cover and refrigerate overnight or bake immediately.
3. Heat the oven to 350°F. Whisk the quinoa mixture making sure it doesn't settle in the bottom.
4. Cover the pan with foil and bake until the liquid is absorbed, and the top of the quinoa is set, for about 60-90 minutes.
5. Turn the oven to high broil, uncover the pan, sprinkle with sliced almonds, and lightly press them into the quinoa.
6. Broil until the almonds just turn golden brown, for about 2-4 minutes, watching closely, as they burn quickly. Allow cooling for 10 minutes then slice the quinoa cake.
7. Distribute the quinoa bake among the containers, and store it in the fridge for 3-4 days.

Nutritions: Calories: 213; Carbs: 41 g; Fat: 4 g; Protein: 5 g

21. SUN-DRIED TOMATOES, DILL, AND FETA OMELET CASSEROLE

Preparation Time
15 minutes

Cooking Time
40 minutes

Servings
6

INGREDIENTS

- 12 large eggs
- 2 cup whole milk
- 8 oz fresh spinach
- 2 garlic cloves, minced
- 12 oz artichoke salad with olives and peppers, drained and chopped
- 5 oz sun-dried tomato Feta cheese, crumbled
- 1 tbsp fresh chopped dill or 1 tsp dried dill
- 1 tsp dried oregano
- 1 tsp lemon pepper
- 1 tsp salt
- 4 tsp olive oil, divided

DIRECTIONS

1. Preheat the oven to 375°F. Chop the fresh dill and artichoke salad. In a skillet over medium heat, add 1 tbsp olive oil.
2. Sauté the spinach and garlic until wilted, about 3 minutes. Oil a 9x13-inch baking dish and layer the spinach and artichoke salad evenly in the dish.
3. In a medium bowl, whisk together the eggs, milk, herbs, salt, and lemon pepper. Pour the egg mixture over vegetables and sprinkle with Feta cheese.
4. Bake in the center of the oven for 35–40 minutes until firm in the center. Allow to cool, slice, and distribute among the storage containers. Store for 2–3 days or freeze for 3 months.

Nutritions: Calories: 196; Carbohydrates: 5 g; Fat: 12 g; Protein: 10 g

22. BREAKFAST TACO SCRAMBLE

Preparation Time
15 minutes

Cooking Time
1 hour and 25 minutes

Servings
4

INGREDIENTS

- Cooking spray
- 8 large eggs, beaten
- ¼ tsp seasoning salt
- 1 lb 99% lean ground turkey
- 2 tbsp Greek seasoning
- ½ small onion, minced
- 2 tbsp bell pepper, minced
- 4 oz can of tomato sauce
- ¼ cup water
- ¼ cup chopped scallions or cilantro, for topping

For the potatoes:
- 12 (1 lb) baby gold or red potatoes, quartered
- 4 tsp olive oil
- ¾ tsp salt
- ½ tsp garlic powder
- Fresh black pepper, to taste

DIRECTIONS

1. In a large bowl, beat the eggs and season with seasoning salt. Preheat the oven to 425°F. Spray a 9x12 or large oval casserole dish with cooking oil.
2. Add the potatoes 1 tbsp oil, ¾ tsp salt, garlic powder, and black pepper, and toss to coat. Bake for 45 minutes to 1 hour, tossing every 15 minutes.
3. In the meantime, brown the turkey in a large skillet over medium heat, breaking it up while it cooks. Once no longer pink, add in the Greek seasoning.
4. Add in the bell pepper, onion, tomato sauce, and water, stir and cover, and simmer on low for about 20 minutes. Spray a different skillet with nonstick spray over medium heat.
5. Once heated, add in the eggs seasoned with ¼ tsp salt and scramble for 2-3 minutes, or cook until it sets.
6. Distribute ¾ cup turkey and ⅔ cup eggs and divide the potatoes in each storage container, store for 3-4 days.

Nutritions: Calories: 450; Fat: 19 g; Carbs: 24.5 g; Protein: 46 g

23. GREEN PROTEIN PAPAYA SMOOTHIE

Preparation Time
5 minutes

Cooking Time
0 minutes

Servings
2

INGREDIENTS

- 1 kiwi
- 1 banana
- ¼ cup papaya
- 2 celery stalks
- 2 cup kale
- 1 cup water

DIRECTIONS

1. Put all ingredients in a blender and blend until smooth.

Nutritions: Calories: 156.9; Total fat: 1.0 g; Saturated fat: 0.2 g; Polyunsaturated fat: 0.3 g; Monounsaturated fat: 0.1 g; Cholesterol: 0.0 mg; Sodium: 54.7 mg; Potassium: 941.2 mg; Total carbohydrates: 38.3 g; Dietary fiber: 6.5 g; Sugar: 20.7 g; Protein: 3.6 g

24. OATMEAL WITH FRUIT AND NUTS

Preparation Time 5 minutes   **Cooking Time** 5 minutes   **Servings** 2

INGREDIENTS

- ½ cup oats
- 1 cup almond milk
- ¼ cup sour cream
- ¼ cup fruit of your choice, diced
- 1 tbsp nuts of your choice

DIRECTIONS

1. Mix the oats and almond milk in a small pan and bring to a boil over high heat.
2. Turn the heat to medium and simmer it, stirring well for about 4-5 minutes, till the oats are cooked.
3. Remove from heat, cover it, and leave it on one side for 2 minutes.
4. Serve with sour cream, your choice of fruit, and nuts.

Nutritions: Calories: 116.0; Total fat: 1.8 g; Saturated fat: 0.3 g; Polyunsaturated fat: 0.7 g; Monounsaturated fat: 0.6 g; Cholesterol: 0.0 mg; Sodium: 207.0 mg; Potassium: 112.0 mg; Total carbohydrates: 23.5 g; Dietary fiber: 2.1 g; Sugar: 0.0 g; Protein: 2.8 g

25. MAGIC OF VEGETABLE PANCAKES

Preparation Time
15 minutes

Cooking Time
10 minutes

Servings
4

INGREDIENTS

- ¼ cup all-purpose flour
- ¼ tsp baking powder
- ¼ tsp salt
- ¼ tsp pepper
- 1 cup applesauce
- ⅛ cup milk
- ½ cup grated carrots
- ½ cup grated zucchini
- 1 green onion, sliced
- 1 tbsp oil

DIRECTIONS

1. In a bowl, combine flour, baking powder, salt, and pepper. In another bowl mix applesauce, milk, carrots, zucchini, and onions. Add these to the dry ingredients and stir until combined.
2. Heat 1 tbsp oil over medium heat with a large pan. Pour the mixture with a spoon into the pan and make a few pancakes at once.
3. Cook on each side for about 2 minutes. Add the remaining oil to the pan as needed. Serve the pancakes at the same time.

Nutritions: Calories: 198.2; Total fat: 6.2 g; Saturated fat: 1.2 g; Polyunsaturated fat: 0.4 g; Monounsaturated fat: 3.8 g; Cholesterol: 2.5 mg; Sodium: 379.0 mg; Potassium: 369.6 mg; Total carbohydrates: 30.4 g; Dietary fiber: 5.9 g; Sugar: 5.0 g; Protein: 8.6 g

26. BRUNCH-STYLE PORTOBELLO MUSHROOMS

Preparation Time
10 minutes

Cooking Time
20 minutes

Servings
4

INGREDIENTS

- 4 large Portobello mushrooms, stems removed
- 2 packages of frozen creamed spinach, thawed (10 oz each)
- 4 large eggs
- ¼ cup shredded Gouda cheese
- ½ cup crumbled cooked bacon
- Salt and pepper, optional

DIRECTIONS

1. Place the mushrooms, stem side up, in a 15x10x1-inch baking pan that hasn't been buttered. Build up the sides of the mushrooms with spinach.
2. Crack an egg carefully into the middle of each mushroom, then top with bacon and cheese. Preheat the oven to 375°F and bake for 18–20 minutes, or until eggs are set.
3. If desired, season with salt and pepper.

Nutritions: Calories: 168; Protein: 12 g; Carbohydrates: 4 g; Fat: 11 g; Cholesterol: 108 mg; Fiber: 1 g

27. PEAR-BLUEBERRY GRANOLA

Preparation Time
15 minutes

Cooking Time
3 hours

Servings
10

INGREDIENTS

- 2 cup fresh or frozen unsweetened blueberries
- 5 medium pears, peeled and thinly sliced
- ½ cup packed brown sugar
- 1 tbsp all-purpose flour
- ⅓ cup apple cider or unsweetened apple juice
- 2 tbsp butter
- 1 tbsp lemon juice
- 3 cup granola without raisins
- 2 tsp ground cinnamon

DIRECTIONS

1. Combine all ingredients in a 4-quart Slow Cooker except granola and butter.
2. Make a butter smear and sprinkle granola on top.
3. Cook for 3-4 hours on low, or until fruit is soft.

Nutritions: Calories: 267; Protein: 7 g; Carbohydrates: 51 g; Fat: 7 g; Cholesterol: 6 mg; Fiber: 10 g

28. BAGEL AVOCADO TOAST

Preparation Time 5 minutes

Cooking Time 5 minutes

Servings 1

INGREDIENTS

- 1 slice of whole-grain bread, toasted
- ¼ medium avocado, mashed
- A pinch of flaky sea salt (Malden)
- 2 tsp Everything Bagel seasoning

DIRECTIONS

1. Spread avocado on the toast.
2. Season it with salt and seasoning.

Nutritions: Calories: 172; Protein: 5.4 g; Carbohydrates: 17.8 g; Fat: 9.8 g; Cholesterol: 2 mg; Fiber: 5.9 g

29. TROPICAL YOGURT

Preparation Time 5 minutes

Cooking Time 10 minutes

Servings 4

INGREDIENTS

- 1 (8 oz) can of crushed unsweetened pineapple; drained
- ¼ tsp grated lime zest
- 2 cup reduced-fat plain yogurt
- ¼ tsp coconut extract
- 2 tsp sugar

DIRECTIONS

1. Combine all ingredients in a small bowl.
2. Chill until ready to serve.

Nutritions: Calories: 121; Protein: 7 g; Carbohydrates: 20 g; Fat: 2 g; Cholesterol: 7 mg; Fiber: 0 g

30. SMOKED SALMON BREAKFAST WRAPS

Preparation Time
1 minutes

Cooking Time
0 minutes

Servings
4

INGREDIENTS

- 1 tbsp snipped fresh chives
- ⅓ cup light cream cheese spread
- 1 tsp lemon peel, finely shredded
- 4 (6-7-inch) whole wheat flour tortillas
- 1 tbsp lemon juice
- 3 oz smoked salmon (lox-style), thinly sliced and cut into strips
- 4 lemon wedges
- 1 small zucchini, trimmed

DIRECTIONS

1. Cream together chives, lemon peel, cream cheese, and lemon juice in a small bowl until creamy. Leave a ½-inch border around the edges of the tortillas after spreading evenly.
2. Distribute the salmon among the tortillas, putting it on the bottom half of each. To make zucchini ribbons, use a sharp vegetable peeler to cut extremely thin slices lengthwise along the zucchini. Serve the fish with zucchini ribbons on top.
3. Tortillas should be rolled up from the bottom up. Slice in half. Serve with lemon wedges if preferred.

Nutritions: Calories: 124; Protein: 11.5 g; Carbohydrates: 14.4 g; Fat: 6 g; Cholesterol: 14.8 mg; Fiber: 8.6 g

31. MIXED-GRAIN MUESLI

Preparation Time: 30 minutes
Cooking Time: 20 minutes
Servings: 4

INGREDIENTS

- 3 tbsp steel-cut oats
- 1 ¼ cup water
- 3 tbsp quick-cooking barley
- 1 tbsp honey
- 3 tbsp cracked wheat
- ½ cup fat-free milk
- ⅛ tsp salt
- ¼ tsp apple pie spice or pumpkin pie spice
- 1 small red-skin apple, cored and chopped
- ¼ cup coarsely chopped pecans, almonds, or walnuts, toasted
- 3 tbsp assorted dried fruit (such as blueberries, snipped plums cranberries, snipped apricots, and dried fruit bits)

DIRECTIONS

1. Combine the oats, barley, water, and cracked wheat in a 2-quart saucepan. Bring to a boil, then turn off the heat. Simmer for 8 minutes, uncovered.
2. Cool for 5 minutes in a medium mixing bowl. Add milk, oats mixture, apple pie spice, honey, and salt. Refrigerate for at least 12 hours or up to 3 days after covering.
3. Transfer the cereal to a medium saucepan to serve. Cook, constantly stirring, over low heat until well heated. Divide the mixture into serving dishes. Add dried fruit and apple. Sprinkle almonds on top.

Tip: It's also possible to eat the cereal cold. Allow 15 minutes for it to come to room temperature before serving. To toast entire nuts or big chunks, lay them on parchment paper in a shallow baking pan. Bake for 5–10 minutes, or until brown, at 350 degrees F, shaking the pan once or twice.

Nutritions: Calories: 203; Protein: 7.4 g; Carbohydrates: 36.4 g; Fat: 4.3 g; Cholesterol: 3.2 mg; Fiber: 4.8 g

32. BREAKFAST PARFAITS

Preparation Time
10 minutes

Cooking Time
0 minutes

Servings
4

INGREDIENTS

- 1 cup fresh or frozen raspberries
- 2 cup pineapple chunks
- 1 cup vanilla yogurt
- ½ cup chopped dates or raisins
- ¼ cup sliced almonds
- 1 cup sliced ripe banana

DIRECTIONS

1. Layer the yogurt, dates, raspberries, pineapple, and banana in 4 parfait glasses or serving plates.
2. Sprinkle the almonds on top.
3. Serve right away.

Nutritions: Calories: 277; Protein: 5 g; Carbohydrates: 60 g; Fat: 4 g; Cholesterol: 3 mg; Fiber: 6 g

33. BLUEBERRY MUFFINS

Preparation Time
15 minutes

Cooking Time
25 minutes

Servings
12

INGREDIENTS

- ¼ cup coconut flour
- 1 ¾ cup almond flour
- ¼ tsp baking soda
- 1 tbsp baking powder
- 1 cup blueberries
- 1 ½ tsp vanilla extract
- ¼ tsp salt
- ½ cup reduced-fat milk
- 3 large eggs
- ¼ cup avocado oil
- ⅓ cup and 2 tbsp light brown sugar
- Cooking spray

DIRECTIONS

1. Preheat the oven to 350°F. Using cooking spray, generously coat a muffin tray. Sift together coconut flour, baking soda, almond flour, baking powder, and salt in a large mixing bowl. Toss in the blueberries to coat.
2. Whisk the brown sugar, eggs, oil, milk, and vanilla extract in a medium mixing bowl. Stir in the wet ingredients until well blended. Using roughly ¼ cup batter per muffin cup, divide the batter among muffin cups.
3. Bake the muffins for 20-25 minutes, or until it turns light brown around the edges and the toothpick inserted in the middle comes out clean. Allow it cool for 20 minutes in a pan on a wire rack. Remove it from the tin and let cool thoroughly.

Nutritions: Calories: 204; Protein: 5.8 g; Carbohydrates: 14.9 g; Fat: 14.6 g; Cholesterol: 47.3 mg; Fiber: 2.9 g

34. CINNAMON STREUSEL ROLLS

Preparation Time 45 minutes | **Cooking Time** 30 minutes | **Servings** 15

INGREDIENTS

- 2 tsp packed brown sugar
- ¼ tsp vanilla extract
- 1 cup + 2-3 tsp fat-free milk, divided
- 4 tbsp tub-style 60-70% vegetable oil spread, divided
- ¼ cup warm water (110-115 degrees F)
- 1 tsp salt
- 4-4 ½ cup all-purpose flour
- ¼ cup powdered sugar
- 1 package of active dry yeast
- ½ cup rolled oats, toasted
- ¼ cup refrigerated or frozen egg product; thawed or 1 egg, lightly beaten
- 2 tsp ground cinnamon
- ⅓ cup light sour cream
- ¼ cup chopped pecans, toasted

DIRECTIONS

1. In a small saucepan, heat and whisk 1 cup milk, 2 tbsp vegetable oil spread, brown sugar, and salt just until heated (110-115 degrees F); leave aside. In a large mixing bowl, combine the warm water and yeast; set aside for 10 minutes. Toss the yeast mixture with the egg and milk mixture. With a wooden spoon, stir in the flour substitute and as much of the leftover all-purpose flour as you can.
2. On a lightly floured surface, roll out the dough. Knead in enough residual flour to form a soft, smooth, and elastic dough (3-5 minutes total). Form a ball out of the dough. Turn once to coat the surface and place in a lightly oiled bowl. Allow rising until doubled in size in a warm location (about 1 hour). Punch the dough down. Turn the dough out onto a floured board. Cover and set aside for 10 minutes to allow flavors to meld.
3. Meanwhile, carefully oil and put aside a 13x9-inch baking pan. In a medium mixing bowl, combine the oats and cinnamon. Blend in the remaining 2 tbsp vegetable oil distributed with your fingertips until the mixture is crumbly. Add the pecans and mix well.
4. Make a 15x8-inch rectangle out of the dough. Sprinkle the pecan mixture over one of the long sides, leaving a 1-inch gap. Begin rolling up the long side with the topping in a spiral. Pinch the seam of the dough to seal it, then cut it into 15 equal pieces. Arrange the pieces in a prepared baking pan, cut-sides up. Allow rising until almost doubled in size in a warm place (about 30 minutes).
5. Preheat the oven to 375°F and bake for 25-30 minutes, or until golden brown. Cool for 5 minutes in the pan on a wire rack. Meanwhile, whisk together the sour cream, vanilla, powdered sugar, and 2-3 tbsp milk to make a drizzling consistency. Take the rolls out of the pan. Drizzle frosting on top. Warm the dish before serving.

Nutritions: Calories: 194; Protein: 5.2 g; Carbohydrates: 32.5 g; Fat: 4.8 g; Cholesterol: 1.8 mg; Fiber: 3.3 g

35. APPLE CINNAMON CHIA PUDDING

Preparation Time
10 minutes

Cooking Time
0 minutes

Servings
1

INGREDIENTS

- 2 tbsp chia seeds
- ½ cup unsweetened almond milk or other non-dairy milk
- ¼ tsp vanilla extract
- 2 tsp pure maple syrup
- ¼ tsp ground cinnamon
- 1 tbsp chopped toasted pecans, divided
- ½ cup diced apple, divided

DIRECTIONS

1. Combine chia, vanilla, almond milk (non-dairy milk), maple syrup, and cinnamon in a small bowl. Refrigerate for approximately 8 hours and for up to 3 days after covering.
2. When ready for serving, give it a good stir. Half of the pudding should be spooned into 1 serving glass (or bowl), followed by half of the apple and pecans.
3. Top with the remaining apple and pecans and the remainder of the pudding.

Nutritions: Calories: 233; Protein: 4.8 g; Carbohydrates: 27.7 g; Fat: 12.7 g; Cholesterol: 1 mg; Fiber: 10.1 g

36. WATERMELON AND BERRY SALAD WITH BUCKWHEAT

Preparation Time
10 minutes

Cooking Time
5 minutes

Servings
4

INGREDIENTS

- 800 g seedless watermelon, skin removed and cut into wedges
- 2 tbsp pistachios, coarsely chopped
- 250 g strawberries, hulled, halved
- 2 tbsp shredded coconut
- ⅔ cup natural yogurt to serve
- 2 tbsp raw buckwheat kernels
- 125 g fresh raspberries

DIRECTIONS

1. Preheat the oven to 180°C/160°C fan-forced. Line a baking pan using baking paper.
2. In a mixing dish, combine the coconut, buckwheat, and pistachios. Spread buckwheat mixture evenly over the prepared baking pan and bake for 5 minutes, stirring once, or until light brown.
3. On serving plates, arrange the strawberry, watermelon, and raspberries. Top each with a dollop of yogurt and a sprinkle of the buckwheat mixture.

Nutritions: Calories: 189; Protein: 7 g; Carbohydrates: 22 g; Fat: 7 g; Cholesterol: 1 mg; Fiber: 5 g

37. HEALTHY BREAKFAST MUFFINS

Preparation Time
10 minutes

Cooking Time
20 minutes

Servings
6

INGREDIENTS

- ½ cup moist coconut flakes
- ¾ cup whole meal flour
- ½ cup coconut sugar
- ¾ cup plain flour
- ½ cup milk
- 2 tsp baking powder
- ⅓ cup light olive oil
- ½ cup passionfruit, warmed mango, and chia jam, warmed
- 1 egg, lightly whisked

DIRECTIONS

1. Preheat the oven to 180°F/160°F fan force. A baking paper should be used to line 6 (200 ml) muffin holes.
2. Whisk together the coconut sugar, coconut flakes, flours, and baking powder using a whisk. In the middle, dig a well. Add oil, milk, and egg.
3. Mix everything with a large metal spoon until it's just blended. Add the jam and mix well.
4. Fill muffin tins halfway with the mixture. Bake for 15-18 minutes, or until a skewer inserted in the middle comes out clean on one of the muffins.
5. Allow cooling before serving. Brush with passionfruit, warmed mango, and chia jam, if desired.

Nutritions: Calories: 175; Protein: 4.5 g; Carbohydrates: 24 g; Fat: 7 g; Cholesterol: 32 mg; Fiber: 2.1 g

38. TURKEY BREAKFAST SAUSAGE

Preparation Time
10 minutes

Cooking Time
10 minutes

Servings
8

INGREDIENTS

- ¼ tsp black pepper
- 1 lb ground turkey
- ¾ tsp dried sage
- ¼ tsp white pepper
- ½ tsp garlic powder
- ¼ tsp ground mace
- ¼ tsp onion powder
- 1 tsp olive oil
- ¼ tsp ground allspice

DIRECTIONS

1. Mix all the ingredients well. Preheat the oven to 325°F and fry, grill, or bake on a prepared baking sheet until desired doneness or 10 minutes.

Nutritions: Calories: 69; Protein: 13 g; Carbohydrates: 1 g; Fat: 7 g; Cholesterol: 41 mg; Fiber: 0 g

39. VEGETABLE OMELET

Preparation Time: 5 minutes

Cooking Time: 5 minutes

Servings: 2

INGREDIENTS

- ¼ cup onion, diced
- 1 tbsp olive oil
- ¼ cup green bell peppers, diced
- 2 oz mushrooms, sliced
- ¼ cup zucchini, sliced
- 2 tbsp fat-free sour cream
- ½ cup tomato, diced
- 2 oz Swiss cheese, shredded
- 1 cup egg substitute
- 2 tbsp water
- Nonstick veggie spray

DIRECTIONS

1. In a large pan, heat the olive oil and cook the mushrooms, zucchini, green bell pepper, onion, and tomato until tender.
2. Combine the sour cream egg substitute, and whisk until frothy. Place an omelet pan or skillet over medium-high heat and coat with the nonstick veggie spray.
3. Fill the pan with the egg mixture. As it cooks, lift the sides to enable the raw egg to flow below. Cover half of the eggs with cheese and sautéed veggies when almost set, then fold another half over. Cook the eggs until they are set.

Nutritions: Calories: 263; Protein: 25 g; Carbohydrates: 8 g; Fat: 13 g; Cholesterol: 17 mg; Fiber: 2 g

40. BREAKFAST POTATOES

Preparation Time: 5 minutes
Cooking Time: 15 minutes
Servings: 6

INGREDIENTS

- ¼ cup green bell peppers, chopped
- 1 cup onion, chopped
- 4 potatoes
- ½ tsp freshly ground black pepper
- 1 tbsp unsalted margarine

DIRECTIONS

1. Boil or microwave the potatoes until nearly done. Drain them and coarsely chop them and combine them with onion and green bell pepper. In a wide skillet, melt margarine.
2. Toss in the potato mixture. Add a pinch of black pepper to the top. Fry till golden brown, flipping often.

Nutritions: Calories: 201; Protein: 5 g; Carbohydrates: 42 g; Fat: 2 g; Cholesterol: 0 mg; Fiber: 5 g

41. COUSCOUS CEREAL WITH FRUIT

Preparation Time: 5 minutes
Cooking Time: 5 minutes
Servings: 2

INGREDIENTS

- 2 tbsp raisins
- ½ cup couscous
- ¾ cup water
- 2 tbsp dried cranberries
- ½ tsp cinnamon
- 1 tbsp honey

DIRECTIONS

1. Bring a pot of water to a gentle boil.
2. Stir in the couscous, then cover and remove from the heat.
3. Allow for a 5-minute rest period. Add the remaining ingredients.

Nutritions: Calories: 250; Protein: 6 g; Carbohydrates: 57 g; Fat: 2 g; Cholesterol: 0 mg; Fiber: 3 g

42. FRENCH TOAST

Preparation Time: 5 minutes
Cooking Time: 15 minutes
Servings: 4

INGREDIENTS

- ¾ cup skim milk
- ½ cup egg substitute
- 2 tsp vanilla extract
- 8 slices of day-old, whole wheat bread
- ½ tsp cinnamon
- Nonstick vegetable oil spray

DIRECTIONS

1. Whisk the egg substitute, vanilla, milk, and cinnamon in a large mixing bowl or dish. Dip both sides of the bread into the egg mixture.
2. Place a griddle or nonstick skillet over medium-high heat and coat with the nonstick vegetable oil spray.
3. Cook for at least 3 minutes on each side, or until both sides of bread are golden brown, on a pan or skillet.

Nutritions: Calories: 185; Protein: 11 g; Carbohydrates: 27 g; Fat: 3 g; Cholesterol: 1 mg; Fiber: 2 g

43. PASTA FRITTATA

Preparation Time: 10 minutes
Cooking Time: 20 minutes
Servings: 4

INGREDIENTS

- 1 cup onion, chopped
- 2 tbsp olive oil
- 1 cup red bell pepper, diced
- 2 cup cooked pasta
- 1 cup egg substitute
- ¼ cup grated Parmesan

DIRECTIONS

1. Preheat a broiler-safe nonstick skillet with a 10-inch (25-cm) diameter.
2. When the pan is heated, add the oil, and cook the red bell pepper and onion, stirring regularly, for 2-3 minutes. Toss the pasta into the pan and toss thoroughly.
3. Flatten the pasta onto the pan's bottom using a spatula when all the ingredients are fully mixed. Allow it to simmer for a few more minutes.
4. Whisk the egg substitute and the grated Parmesan cheese in a separate bowl.
5. Pour the egg mixture over the pasta, ensuring the egg is equally distributed.
6. Lift the edges of the pasta gently to allow the egg to pour beneath and coat the pasta fully. Allow 6-9 minutes for the eggs to cook.
7. Finish cooking by placing the pan on the hot broiler.

Nutritions: Calories: 360; Protein: 18 g; Carbohydrates: 46 g; Fat: 12 g; Cholesterol: 6 mg; Fiber: 3 g

44. OVERNIGHT CHERRY-ALMOND OATMEAL

Preparation Time: 10 minutes
Cooking Time: 7 hours
Servings: 6

INGREDIENTS

- 1 cup steel-cut oats
- 4 cup vanilla almond milk
- ⅓ cup packed brown sugar
- 1 cup dried cherries
- ½ tsp salt
- Additional almond milk (optional)
- ½ tsp ground cinnamon
- Cooking spray

DIRECTIONS

1. Combine all ingredients in a 3-quart Slow Cooker covered with cooking spray.
2. Cook on low for 7–8 hours, covered until oats are soft. Before serving, give it a good stir.
3. Serve with more milk if desired.

Nutritions: Calories: 276; Protein: 5 g; Carbohydrates: 57 g; Fat: 4 g; Cholesterol: 0 mg; Fiber: 4 g

45. BANANA OATMEAL PANCAKES

Preparation Time: 10 minutes
Cooking Time: 5 min./batch
Servings: 8

INGREDIENTS

- 1 large firm banana, finely chopped
- 2 cup complete whole wheat, pancake mix
- ¼ cup chopped walnuts
- ½ cup old-fashioned oats
- Cooking spray

DIRECTIONS

1. Follow the package instructions for making the pancake batter. Add the oats, bananas, and walnuts.
2. Pour ¼ cupsful of batter onto a heated griddle covered with cooking spray; flip when bubbles appear on the surface.
3. Cook until golden brown on the second side.

Nutritions: Calories: 155; Protein: 7 g; Carbohydrates: 28 g; Fat: 4 g; Cholesterol: 0 mg; Fiber: 4 g

46. GARLIC-HERB MINI QUICHES

Preparation Time: 25 minutes
Cooking Time: 0 minutes
Servings: 45

INGREDIENTS

- ¼ cup fat-free milk
- 1 (6 ½ oz) package of garlic-herb reduced-fat spreadable cheese
- 3 (1.9 oz each) packages of frozen miniature, phyllo tart shells
- 2 large eggs
- Minced chives (optional)
- 2 tbsp minced fresh parsley

DIRECTIONS

1. Preheat the oven to 350°F. Beat the spreadable cheese, milk, and eggs in a small bowl. Fill each tart shell with 2 tsp the mixture and place on an ungreased baking sheet. Serve with a parsley garnish.
2. Bake for 10–12 minutes, or until the filling has set and the shells have browned somewhat. If desired, garnish with chives. Warm the dish before serving.

Nutritions: Calories: 31; Protein: 1 g; Carbohydrates: 2 g; Fat: 2 g; Cholesterol: 12 mg; Fiber: 0 g

47. YOGURT AND HONEY FRUIT CUPS

Preparation Time: 10 minutes
Cooking Time: 0 minutes
Servings: 6

INGREDIENTS

- ¾ cup vanilla, mandarin orange, or lemon yogurt
- 4 ½ cup cut-up fresh fruit (apples, pears, grapes, bananas, etc.)
- 1 tbsp honey
- ¼ tsp almond extract
- ½ tsp grated orange zest

DIRECTIONS

1. Fruit should be divided into 6 separate serving bowls.
2. Toss the fruit with orange zest, yogurt, honey, and extract.

Nutritions: Calories: 97; Protein: 2 g; Carbohydrates: 23 g; Fat: 0 g; Cholesterol: 2 mg; Fiber: 2 g

48. OATMEAL WAFFLES

Preparation Time
25 minutes

Cooking Time
10 minutes

Servings
10 waffles

INGREDIENTS

- ½ cup whole wheat flour
- 1 cup all-purpose flour
- 2 packets of instant maple and brown sugar or apple cinnamon oatmeal
- ¼ tsp salt
- 1 tbsp baking powder
- 1 ½ cup 2% milk
- 1 tsp ground cinnamon
- ⅓ cup butter; melted
- 2 eggs
- ½ cup chopped pecans or walnuts

DIRECTIONS

1. In a large mixing basin, combine the dry ingredients. In a separate bowl, whisk together the eggs, milk, and butter. Stir in the wet ingredients just until the dry ingredients are moistened.
2. At this time, folded in the pecans. In a preheated waffle iron, bake until golden brown, according to the manufacturer's instructions. Serve with a dollop of maple syrup on the side.

Nutritions: Calories: 205.9; Protein: 10.4 g; Carbohydrates: 30.0 g; Fat: 5.2 g; Cholesterol: 55.3 mg; Fiber: 4.3 g

49. CHICKEN AND ASPARAGUS CREPES

Preparation Time
1 hour + chilling time

Cooking Time
20 minutes

Servings
12

INGREDIENTS

- 2 tbsp butter, melted
- 3 eggs
- 1 ½ cup 2% milk
- ¼ tsp salt
- 1 cup all-purpose flour

For the filling:
- 1 tsp canola oil
- 1 ½ cup cut fresh asparagus (1-inch pieces)
- 1 small onion; chopped
- 3 cup cubed rotisserie chicken
- 2 ½ cup sliced fresh mushrooms

For the sauce:
- ⅛ tsp pepper
- ¼ tsp salt
- 1 ½ cup 2% milk
- ¼ cup all-purpose flour
- ⅔ cup part-skim shredded mozzarella cheese
- ¼ cup butter, cubed
- 6 slices of Swiss cheese, halved

DIRECTIONS

1. Whisk the milk, eggs, and butter in a large mixing bowl. Combine the flour and salt; add to the egg mixture and combine well. Refrigerate it for 1 hour.
2. Over medium heat, gently butter an 8-inch nonstick pan and pour ¼ cup of batter into the middle. Lift and tilt the pan to evenly coat the bottom. Cook until the top seems dry, then flip and cook for another 15–20 seconds. Place on a wire rack to cool. Continue with the remaining batter, re-greasing the skillet as necessary. When the crepes are cold, layer them with waxed paper/paper towels between them.
3. In a skillet, sauté the asparagus and onion with canola oil until they are soft. Cook for another 2 minutes after adding the mushrooms. Remove the pan from the heat and add the chicken. Set it aside.
4. Melt the butter in a small pot over medium heat for the sauce. Stir in the salt, flour, and pepper until smooth, then add the milk in a slow, steady stream. Bring to a boil, then reduce to low heat and simmer, constantly stirring, for 2 minutes, or until the sauce has thickened.
5. Fill each crepe halfway with filling, then top with the 2 tbsp sauce and 1 slice of Swiss cheese. Roll up and lay in 2 greased 11x7-inch baking trays, seam side down. Sprinkle Mozzarella cheese on top. Bake for 20–25 minutes, uncovered, at 350°F, or until bubbling.

Nutritions: Calories: 394.9; Protein: 22.3 g; Carbohydrates: 17.6 g; Fat: 23.1 g; Cholesterol: 140 mg; Fiber: 2 g

50. BANANA OAT BREAKFAST COOKIES

Preparation Time
20 minutes

Cooking Time
15 minutes

Servings
12

INGREDIENTS

- ½ cup chunky peanut butter
- 1 cup mashed ripe bananas (about 2 medium)
- ½ cup honey
- 1 cup old-fashioned oats
- 1 tsp vanilla extract
- ¼ cup nonfat dry milk powder
- ½ cup whole wheat flour
- ½ tsp salt
- 2 tsp ground cinnamon
- 1 cup dried cranberries/raisins
- ¼ tsp baking soda

DIRECTIONS

1. Preheat the oven to 350°F. Blend bananas, honey, peanut butter, and vanilla in a mixing bowl until smooth. In a separate dish, whisk together dry ingredients; gradually fold into the wet mixture. Add the dried cranberries and mix well. Drop the dough by ¼ cupsful onto prepared baking sheets, 3 inches apart, and flatten to ½-inch thickness.
2. Bake for 14-16 minutes, or until golden brown. Allow 5 minutes for cooling on the pans. Place on wire racks to cool. Serve warm or at room temperature. Microwave the cookie on high for 15-20 seconds or until warm to reheat enough.

Nutritions: Calories: 212; Protein: 5 g; Carbohydrates: 38 g; Fat: 6 g; Cholesterol: 38 mg; Fiber: 4 g

LUNCH

51. COCONUT AND PEANUT AUBERGINE CURRY

Preparation Time
15 minutes

Cooking Time
15 minutes

Servings
2

INGREDIENTS

- Oil for frying
- 1 aubergine or eggplant, cut into large chunks
- 1 onion, chopped
- 1 garlic clove, crushed
- 1 (5 cm) piece of ginger, finely grated
- 1 tsp cumin
- ½ tsp coriander seeds, crushed
- ½ tsp turmeric
- ¼ tsp chili powder
- 1 cup half-fat coconut milk
- ½ tbsp tamarind paste
- ½ tbsp peanut butter
- Coriander
- Bread or rice to serve

DIRECTIONS

1. Heat 1 tbsp oil in a pan. Fry eggplant in batches until they are golden brown and soft. If necessary, add another spoonful of oil. Put on one side until needed.
2. Add the onion to the same pan and cook until it becomes smooth and golden.
3. Add garlic and ginger and cook for a minute.
4. Add the spices and cook for 2 minutes.
5. Add coconut milk, tamarind, and peanut butter. Cook over low heat until peanut butter dissolves.
6. Add the eggplant and simmer for 15 minutes. Stir in the coriander and serve with bread or rice.

Nutritions: Calories: 235.5; Total fat: 10.2 g; Saturated fat: 4.1 g; Polyunsaturated fat: 2.0 g; Monounsaturated fat: 3.4 g; Cholesterol: 0.0 mg; Sodium: 969.1 mg; Potassium: 548.9 mg; Total carbohydrates: 33.3 g; Dietary fiber: 7.2 g; Sugar: 1.7 g; Protein: 5.7 g

52. ORANGE BELL PEPPERS CURRY

Preparation Time
35 minutes

Cooking Time
15 minutes

Servings
3

INGREDIENTS

- 1 tbsp oil
- 1 medium bell pepper
- 2 garlic cloves
- 1 tsp cumin
- ½ tsp paprika
- ½ tsp cayenne pepper
- ½ tsp salt
- ½ small bunch of kale
- 2 cup peas, cooked
- ½ tomatoes
- ½ cup water

DIRECTIONS

1. Heat the oil in a large pan over medium heat.
2. Add the bell peppers and garlic and cook, stirring occasionally for about 10 minutes, until it starts to brown.
3. Add cumin, paprika, cayenne pepper, and salt, and cook for 15 seconds.
4. Add kale. Boil and stir for about 3 minutes.
5. Add peas, tomatoes, and water.
6. Bring to the boil.
7. Reduce the heat and simmer, cover, and cook, stirring occasionally, until the vegetables are soft, for about 10 minutes.

Nutritions: Calories: 29.0; Total fat: 0.3 g; Saturated fat: 0.1 g; Polyunsaturated fat: 0.1 g; Monounsaturated fat: 0.0 g; Cholesterol: 0.0 mg; Sodium: 4.0 mg; Potassium: 260.0 mg; Total carbohydrates: 6.9 g; Dietary fiber: 2.5 g; Sugar: 0.0 g; Protein: 1.3 g

53. ROASTED BROCCOLI WITH LEMON

Preparation Time
10 minutes

Cooking Time
15 minutes

Servings
3

INGREDIENTS

- 1 head broccoli, separated into florets
- 1 tsp extra-virgin olive oil
- ½ tsp sea salt
- ¼ tsp ground black pepper
- ½ garlic clove, minced
- ¼ tsp lemon juice

DIRECTIONS

1. Preheat the oven to 400°F.
2. In a large bowl, mix broccoli flowers with extra-virgin olive oil, sea salt, pepper, and garlic. Spread the broccoli in a uniform layer on a baking sheet.
3. Bake until the florets are sufficiently tender to pierce the stems with a fork, about 15-20 minutes.
4. Remove and place in a serving bowl. Squeeze lemon juice over the broccoli before serving to get a refreshing and acidic finish.

Nutritions: Calories: 74.5; Total fat: 5.1 g; Saturated fat: 0.7 g; Polyunsaturated fat: 0.7 g; Monounsaturated fat: 3.4 g; Cholesterol: 0.0 mg; Sodium: 624.5 mg; Potassium: 333.3 mg; Total carbohydrates: 6.6 g; Dietary fiber: 3.3 g; Sugar: 0.2 g; Protein: 3.0 g

54. TOFU AND KALE SANDWICH

Preparation Time
10 minutes

Cooking Time
25 minutes

Servings
2

INGREDIENTS

For the vegan kale pesto:
- 1 ½ handful of kale
- ¼ cup walnuts
- 1 garlic clove
- 1 ½ tbsp nutritional yeast
- 3 tbsp olive oil
- ¼ tsp Italian spice mixture (oregano, basil, rosemary, thyme, and sage)
- Salt to taste
- Black pepper to taste

For the sandwiches:
- 4 oz smoked tofu (alternatively, you can also use marinated regular tofu)
- ½ small zucchini, cut into slices
- ½ carrot
- Lettuce
- 2 whole wheat buns
- ½ tsp soy sauce (optional)
- Salt, pepper, and Italian spices to taste
- Olive oil for frying

DIRECTIONS

1. First, prepare the kale pesto by putting all the ingredients in a food processor and mixing everything together.
2. Then, cut the tofu into thin strips. Heat some olive oil in a medium pan and fry the tofu on each side for about 2-3 minutes until golden brown and crispy. If you want, you can also add about ½ tsp soy sauce. Once you have finished the tofu, set it aside.
3. Heat a little more olive oil and cook the zucchini slices for 3 minutes. Season with salt, pepper, and Italian spices.
4. Cut the whole-wheat buns in half and cover both halves generously with kale pesto. Put lettuce, tofu, carrots, and zucchini on the grill. Wait some minutes, pull them out, and put them inside the sandwich.

Nutritions: Calories: 276.9; Total fat: 9.1 g; Saturated fat: 1.5 g; Polyunsaturated fat: 5.0 g; Monounsaturated fat: 2.1 g; Cholesterol: 0.0 mg; Sodium: 1,035.6 mg; Potassium: 183.1 mg; Total carbohydrates: 33.1 g; Dietary fiber: 3.6 g; Sugar: 12.7 g; Protein: 16.1 g

55. SESAME-GINGER MARINATED VEGETABLES

Preparation Time
10 minutes

Cooking Time
25 minutes

Servings
2

INGREDIENTS

- 1 cup trimmed green bean pieces (1-2-inches)
- 1 cup sliced carrots
- 1 cup small broccoli florets
- Boiling water as necessary
- Iced water as necessary
- ⅛ cup toasted sesame oil
- 3 tbsp rice vinegar
- 1 tbsp soy sauce
- 1 scallion, cut into 1-inch pieces
- 2 tsp minced fresh ginger

DIRECTIONS

1. Cook the green beans, carrots, and broccoli in a small saucepan of boiling water until crisp, from 30 seconds to 1 minute.
2. Take them out of the boiling water with a slotted spoon and put them in a bowl of iced water. Leave them to cool.
3. Drain, dry, and place them in a medium bowl.
4. Whisk the oil, vinegar, soy sauce, scallion, and ginger in a small saucepan and heat until smoking.
5. Pour the marinade over the vegetables.
6. Cover and cool.

Nutritions: Calories: 206.5; Total fat: 10.7 g; Saturated fat: 4.0 g; Polyunsaturated fat: 1.3 g; Monounsaturated fat: 4.3 g; Cholesterol: 5.7 mg; Sodium: 464.3 mg; Potassium: 452.7 mg; Total carbohydrates: 2.5 g; Dietary fiber: 0.3 g; Sugar: 0.4 g; Protein: 23.8 g

56. TOFU AND VEGETABLE CURRY

Preparation Time: 10 minutes
Cooking Time: 15 minutes
Servings: 2

INGREDIENTS

- ½ tbsp olive oil
- 2 cup tofu, cut into cubes
- ½ large red onion, finely chopped
- 1 tbsp curry paste
- 1 can lite almond milk
- ½ cup acorns, peeled, seeded, diced
- 1 cup water
- ¼ cup cauliflower, trimmed, cut into florets
- ⅛ green beans, trimmed, sliced
- ½ cup tomatoes, halved
- Coriander sprigs, to serve
- Steamed basmati rice, to serve

DIRECTIONS

1. Heat half of the olive oil in a large saucepan over high heat.
2. Cook the tofu occasionally for 3-4 minutes or until golden brown and transfer to a plate.
3. Heat the remaining oil in the same pan over medium heat.
4. Fry the onion, stirring occasionally for about 3-4 minutes, or until it becomes soft.
5. Add the curry paste and cook. Stir it for 1 minute.
6. Add the almond milk, acorn, and 1 cup water. Cover and simmer for 5 minutes.
7. Add cauliflower, beans, and tomatoes. Cook over low heat, covered, for 3-4 minutes or until the vegetables are tender.
8. Serve the curry with steamed rice garnished with coriander.

Nutritions: Calories: 240.9; Total fat: 11.9 g; Saturated fat: 1.9 g; Polyunsaturated fat: 4.5 g; Monounsaturated fat: 4.6 g; Cholesterol: 0.0 mg; Sodium: 590.8 mg; Potassium: 428.5 mg; Total carbohydrates: 23.2 g; Dietary fiber: 6.6 g; Sugar: 1.5 g; Protein: 13.3 g

57. PAD THAI

Preparation Time: 15 minutes
Cooking Time: 10 minutes
Servings: 4

INGREDIENTS

- 16 oz dried rice noodles (I prefer Pad Thai noodles)
- Water as needed
- 8 garlic cloves, minced
- 6 tbsp onion, diced
- 4 heads of baby bok choy
- 1 cup soft tofu
- 4 cup bean sprouts
- 4 green onions, sliced
- ½ cup peanuts or cashews, chopped, unsalted, and dry-roasted
- ½ cup fresh coriander
- 6 tbsp oil
- 4 tbsp vegetable stock
- 2 wedges of lime and a little lime juice to taste

For the Pad Thai sauce:
- 1 tbsp tamarind paste
- ½ cup vegetable stock
- 7 tbsp soy sauce
- 2 tsp chili sauce
- 6 tbsp brown sugar

DIRECTIONS

1. Bring a pan of water to a boil over high heat. Put in the rice noodles and stir with a fork. Cook for 4-6 minutes, until the noodles are loose but firm to eat (slightly firmer than al dente).
2. Drain and rinse with cold water.
3. Put the ingredients of the *Thai Pad sauce* in a cup and mix well to dissolve the sugar and tamarind. This sauce should have a very strong taste of sweet and sour at first, then salty and spicy. Add more sugar if it is too sour. Leave aside.
4. Heat a wok or large pan over medium heat. Add 1-2 tbsp oil, and fry the garlic and onions for 1 minute.
5. Add bok choy or white wine. Fry for 2 minutes or until the Bok Choy is light green and softens slightly.
6. Put the ingredients aside and add ½ tbsp more oil to the pan. Add the tofu and fry briefly.
7. When the pan is dry, add a little more oil in the middle and add the drained pasta and ⅓ of the sauce. Stir gently for 1-2 minutes.
8. Keep the heat between medium and high to prevent the noodles from sticking or burning.
9. Add the sauce after 3-6 minutes or until the whole sauce is added and the noodles are tender, soft, and deliciously sticky.
10. Turn off the heat and add the bean sprouts, green onion, and ¾ walnuts. Mix and taste, adding more soy sauce if required. If it's too salty or sweet to taste, add a touch of lime juice. If it is very sour, add a little more sugar.
11. Serve the noodles in a serving bowl. Sprinkle the remaining ground walnuts and fresh coriander. Put freshly sliced lime slices on one side and squeeze over the noodles just before eating.

Nutritions: Calories: 126.7; Total fat: 2.3 g; Saturated fat: 0.0 g; Polyunsaturated fat: 0.0 g; Monounsaturated fat: 0.0 g; Cholesterol: 0.0 mg; Sodium: 0.0 mg; Potassium: 0.0 mg; Total carbohydrates: 23.3 g; Protein: 4.0 g

58. STRIP STEAK QUINOA

Preparation Time
15 minutes

Cooking Time
30 minutes

Servings
4

INGREDIENTS

For the quinoa:
- 1 cup uncooked quinoa
- 12 oz strip steak, fat-trimmed
- ⅛ tsp fine sea salt
- Ground black pepper
- 1 tbsp olive oil
- 1 large iceberg lettuce head, finely chopped
- 2 spring onions, finely chopped
- ⅓ cup pine nuts

For the dressing:
- ¼ cup olive oil
- 3 tbsp apple cider vinegar
- 2 tbsp reduced-sodium tamari
- 2 tbsp organic honey

DIRECTIONS

For the quinoa:
1. Follow the package directions for cooking the quinoa. While it's cooking, place a medium-sized mixing bowl in the freezer. Once the quinoa is done cooking, take the mixing bowl out, and transfer the cooked quinoa to the bowl. Allow cooling for a few minutes.
2. Pat the strip steak dry with a paper towel, and season with fine sea salt and ground black pepper.
3. In a wide pan, warm the olive oil over high heat. When hot, add the strip steak and brown for 5–6 minutes on each side until done to your liking. Place the strip steak on a cutting board, and allow it to rest for 5 minutes, then cut it into thin slices.

For the dressing:
4. In a large mixing bowl, combine the olive oil, apple cider vinegar, tamari, and organic honey, and whisk to incorporate.
5. Add the chopped iceberg lettuce, chopped spring onion, and cooled quinoa. Toss well with the dressing.
6. Serve dishes with strip steak pieces and pine nuts on top.

Nutritions: Calories: 526; Total fat: 29 g; Saturated fat: 5 g; Cholesterol: 58 mg; Sodium: 500 mg; Total carbs: 40 g; Fiber: 5 g; Protein: 30 g

59. DELIGHTFUL STUFFED LAMB WITH PEPPERS

Preparation Time
45 minutes

Cooking Time
60 minutes

Servings
6

INGREDIENTS

- 1 onion, finely diced
- 2 tbsp water + additional for cooking
- 1 ½ lb lamb, ground
- 1 cup grated zucchini
- ¼ cup fresh basil, minced
- 1 tsp salt
- 6 bell peppers, any color, seeded, ribbed, and tops removed and reserved

DIRECTIONS

1. Preheat the oven to 350°F. Sauté the onion in the water in a large pan set over medium heat for 5 minutes, or until soft.
2. Add the ground lamb and zucchini. Cook for 10 minutes by breaking up the meat with a spoon.
3. Stir in the basil and salt. Remove from the heat.
4. Fill a casserole dish with 1 ½ inch of water.
5. Stuff each pepper with an equal amount of the lamb mixture and place them into the dish. Cap each pepper with its reserved top.
6. Place the dish in the preheated oven and bake for 45–50 minutes.

Nutritions: Calories: 182; Fat: 27 g; Saturated fat: 12 g; Protein: 22 g; Total carbs: 12 g; Sodium: 681 mg; Cholesterol: 83 mg

60. CHOPPED LAMBS WITH ROSEMARY

Preparation Time 45 minutes

Cooking Time 7-8 hours

Servings 4-6

INGREDIENTS

- 1 medium onion, sliced
- 2 tsp garlic powder
- 2 tsp rosemary, dried
- 1 tsp sea salt
- ½ tsp thyme leaves, dried
- Freshly ground black pepper
- 8 bone-in lamb chops (approx. 3 lb)
- 2 tbsp balsamic vinegar

DIRECTIONS

1. Line the bottom of the Slow Cooker with the onion slices.
2. Stir together the garlic powder, rosemary, salt, thyme, and pepper in a small bowl. Rub the chops evenly with the spice mixture and place gently in the Slow Cooker.
3. Drizzle the vinegar over the top.
4. Cover the Slow Cooker and set it to low. Cook for 7-8 hours and serve.

Nutritions: Calories: 251; Fat: 14.6 g; Saturated fat: 3.8 g; Protein: 27.3 g; Total carbs: 1.3 g; Sodium: 166 mg; Cholesterol: 85 mg

61. BAKED MACKEREL WITH ARTICHOKES AND ALMONDS

Preparation Time: 15 minutes

Cooking Time: 30 minutes

Servings: 4

INGREDIENTS

- 21 oz mackerel fillets
- 4 artichokes
- 2 tbsp shelled almonds
- 3 tbsp extra-virgin olive oil
- Lemon juice
- Salt to taste

DIRECTIONS

1. To begin, line a large baking pan with baking paper and preheat the oven to 350°F.
2. In the meantime, you can proceed to peel the artichokes, removing the outer leaves and the terminal part of the stems; then, cut the artichokes into slices, put them in a bowl, and cover them with lemon juice; moreover, chop the almonds obtaining some coarse fragments.
3. At this point, place the artichoke slices in the baking pan and cook for 15 minutes.
4. At the end of this cooking time, place the mackerel fillets on top of the artichokes, season with a small amount of salt, and cover the surface with almond granules; then leave to cook for a further 15 minutes.
5. When cooked, dress the fillets with raw extra-virgin olive oil, portion, and serve.

Nutritions: Calories: 336; Total fat: 19 g; Saturated fat: 5 g; Cholesterol: 46 mg; Sodium: 450 mg; Total carbs: 21 g; Fiber: 4 g; Protein: 22 g

62. BAKED TUNA FILLETS ON CREAM OF CARROTS AND PISTACHIOS

Preparation Time
10 minutes

Cooking Time
35 minutes

Servings
4

INGREDIENTS

- 21 oz tuna fillets
- 9 oz carrots
- 2 tbsp shelled pistachios
- 3 tbsp extra-virgin olive oil to taste
- 1 small white onion
- Salt to taste

DIRECTIONS

1. One version of the carrot cream involves cooking the carrot in plenty of water for 10-15 minutes; in the meantime, chop the onion and pistachios coarsely.
2. When cooked, allow the carrots to cool and then chop them into small pieces; place them in a large blender along with the onion, 1 tbsp olive oil, and a small amount of salt; blend until smooth and set aside.
3. Next, place the tuna fillets in a large baking dish (previously covered with a sheet of baking paper), season with a bit of salt, and cover the surface with the chopped pistachios; bake at 180°C for 20 minutes.
4. When cooked, season the tuna by adding the remaining olive oil; then, arrange the fillets on a layer of carrot cream on the plate.

Nutritions: Calories: 208; Total fat: 10 g; Saturated fat: 2 g; Cholesterol: 82 mg; Sodium: 215 mg; Total carbs: 6 g; Net carbs: 3 g; Fiber: 1 g; Protein: 25 g

63. CHICKPEA SOUP

Preparation Time
10 minutes

Cooking Time
25 minutes

Servings
4

INGREDIENTS

- 2 tbsp olive oil
- 6 garlic cloves
- 2 medium onions
- 1 cup green onion
- 1 cup bok choy
- 1 cup parsley
- Few basils leave
- Few thymes sprig
- Few sprigs sage
- ½ summer squash
- ½ yellow squash
- 8 cup chickpea stock
- 1 tsp paprika
- 1 ½ cup chickpeas (skinned)
- 2 tsp red chili flakes
- 40 ml water
- ¼ cup grated cheese

DIRECTIONS

1. In a hot pan add the green onion, bok choy, onion, garlic, parsley, basil, thyme, and sage.
2. Then add the chopped summer squash, yellow squash, and paprika. Add some flakes of pepper, water, chickpeas, and chickpea stock.
3. Cook, stirring all the time until the soup boils then leave to simmer for a few minutes.
4. Fry the remaining chickpeas, peppers, summer squash, and yellow squash in olive oil. Top with grated Cheddar cheese.

Nutritions: Calories: 242.8; Total fat: 6.6 g; Saturated fat: 0.9 g; Polyunsaturated fat: 1.1 g; Monounsaturated fat: 4.1 g; Cholesterol: 0.0 mg; Potassium: 474.7 mg; Total carbohydrates: 38.4 g; Dietary fiber: 7.0 g; Sugar: 3.0 g; Protein: 8.4 g

64. LENTIL SALAD FROM HEAVEN WITH BABY SPINACH

Preparation Time
5 minutes

Cooking Time
10 minutes

Servings
4

INGREDIENTS

- 1 cup Brazil nuts
- 2 onions
- 6 tbsp olive oil
- 2 jalapeño peppers
- 10 dried tomatoes
- 6 slices of whole-wheat bread
- 2 cup lentils, cooked
- 2 handfuls of baby spinach
- 4 tbsp balsamic vinegar
- Salt and pepper to taste

Optional:
- 2 small handfuls of raisins
- 2 tsp honey

DIRECTIONS

1. Grill the Brazil nuts over low heat for about 3 minutes in a pan to maximize the taste. Then put them in the salad bowl.
2. Cut the onions into cubes and sauté in olive oil for about 3 minutes over low heat.
3. Add the jalapeño and dried tomatoes to the pan and fry for another 1-2 minutes.
4. Cut the bread into large croutons.
5. Move the onion mixture into a large bowl and add the remaining oil to the pan and fry the bread until it is crisp.
6. Season with salt and pepper.
7. Wash the baby spinach and add it to the bowl.
8. Add the lentils to the bowl and mix well.
9. Season with salt, pepper, and balsamic vinegar.
10. Serve with the croutons.

Nutritions: Calories: 585; Total fat: 16.0 g; Saturated fat: 0.0 g; Polyunsaturated fat: 0.0 g; Monounsaturated fat: 0.0 g; Cholesterol: 0.0 mg; Potassium: 0.0 mg; Total carbohydrates: 89.0 g; Dietary fiber: 12.0 g; Sugar: 23.0 g; Protein: 28.0 g

65. TOMATO, CHICKPEA, AND SWEET POTATO SOUP

Preparation Time
10 minutes

Cooking Time
25 minutes

Servings
2

INGREDIENTS

- ½ tsp extra-virgin olive oil
- 1 garlic clove, minced
- ½ small white onion, chopped
- ½ orange pepper, diced
- 1 large carrot, diced
- ½ (16 oz) can of chickpeas
- ½ (16 oz) can of diced tomatoes (I prefer fire roasted)
- 1 cup vegetarian stock
- ¼ tsp cumin
- ¼ tsp paprika
- ½ tbsp fresh chopped basil
- ¼ tsp kosher salt
- 1/16 tsp cinnamon
- ½ medium sweet potato, peeled and diced
- Salt and pepper for seasoning
- Fresh chopped basil, for garnish
- ½ sliced avocado, for garnish (optional)

DIRECTIONS

1. Heat the olive oil in a medium saucepan over medium heat. Add the onion, garlic, and salt. Sauté for 2 minutes.
2. Put the diced pepper and carrots in the pan and sauté for 5 minutes more.
3. Add the tomatoes to the pan, then the chickpeas, vegetarian broth, cumin, basil, paprika, cinnamon, and salt. Bring to the boil.
4. Add the diced sweet potatoes.
5. Cover and simmer for 10 minutes or until the potatoes are tender. Taste and add more seasoning if necessary.
6. Serve, with basil and /or avocado slices if required.

Nutritions: Calories: 188.0; Total fat: 3.8 g; Saturated fat: 2.2 g; Polyunsaturated fat: 0.5 g; Monounsaturated fat: 0.3 g; Cholesterol: 0.0 mg; Sodium: 776.2 mg; Potassium: 540.7 mg; Total carbohydrates: 32.4 g; Dietary fiber: 6.7 g; Sugar: 2.4 g; Protein: 6.9 g

66. BUTTERBEANS KALE SALAD

Preparation Time: 10 minutes
Cooking Time: 0 minutes
Servings: 2

INGREDIENTS

- 3 oz kale leaves cut into small pieces
- ½ (14 oz) can of butterbeans
- ½ bell pepper, cut into medium pieces
- 1 tbsp chopped onion
- ½ lemon
- 1/6 cup olive oil
- ⅛ tsp salt
- 1/16 tsp ground black pepper

DIRECTIONS

1. Combine kale, butterbeans, peppers, and onion in a large bowl.
2. Beat the lemon juice, olive oil, salt, and pepper and pour over the butterbean's kale mixture.

Nutritions: Calories: 142.4; Total fat: 7.7 g; Saturated fat: 1.1 g; Polyunsaturated fat: 0.9 g; Monounsaturated fat: 5.2 g; Cholesterol: 0.6 mg; Sodium: 180.9 mg; Potassium: 226.6 mg; Total carbohydrates: 15.4 g; Dietary fiber: 3.1 g; Sugar: 1.3 g; Protein: 5.5 g

67. BEANS AND MILLET SALAD WITH SPINACH AND LEMON

Preparation Time
10 minutes

Cooking Time
20 minutes

Servings
2

INGREDIENTS

For the salad:
- ¼ cup dry beans
- ¼ cup millet
- ⅛ cup onion cut into medium pieces
- ½ avocado diced
- ¼ cup tomatoes
- ⅛ cup fresh coriander
- ⅛ cup raw walnuts
- 2 big lettuces

For the creamy oil-free balsamic vinaigrette:
- ⅛ cup fresh pineapple puree
- 1 tbsp balsamic vinegar
- ½ tbsp lime juice
- ½ tbsp Dijon mustard
- Salt and pepper to taste

DIRECTIONS

1. Beat all the ingredients for the vinaigrette together and keep this aside.
2. Mix the salad, except the lettuce in a medium bowl.
3. When serving, place a large handful of lettuce in another bowl. Sprinkle with vinaigrette.

Nutritions: Calories: 338; Total fat: 13 g; Saturated fat: 2 g; Polyunsaturated fat: 3 g; Monounsaturated fat: 7 g; Sodium: 151 mg; Potassium: 754 mg

Total Carbohydrates: 50 g; Dietary fiber: 13 g; Sugar: 9 g; Protein: 12 g

68. BUTTERNUT SQUASH AND QUINOA MASON JAR SALAD

Preparation Time
12 minutes

Cooking Time
22 minutes

Servings
4

INGREDIENTS

- 1 small acorn
- ½ cup cooked millet
- 12 tomatoes cut into pieces
- 4 cup baby spinach
- 2 onions, sliced
- A handful of walnuts
- 2 tbsp tahini
- 4 tbsp olive oil
- Juice of 4 limes
- 2 tsp garlic powder
- Salt and pepper to taste

DIRECTIONS

1. Peel the acorn and cut it into pieces. Arrange on a baking sheet in a layer, season with garlic powder, salt, and pepper, and bake for 20–25 minutes at 390°F until the acorn is tender and lightly browned. Let it cool down a bit.
2. Meanwhile mix the tahini, olive oil, lime juice, and pepper for the vinaigrette.
3. Arrange the salads in 2 preserving jars. First the vinaigrette, then the acorn cubes.
4. Finally, put the tomatoes, onions, walnuts, and baby spinach on top.

Nutritions: Calories: 367.0; Total fat: 10.1 g; Saturated fat: 2.6 g; Polyunsaturated fat: 0.6 g; Monounsaturated fat: 1.4 g; Cholesterol: 10.4 mg; Sodium: 553.2 mg; Potassium: 207.1 mg; Total carbohydrates: 60.7 g; Dietary fiber: 5.4 g; Sugar: 1.7 g; Protein: 10.1 g

69. SPICY LIME PORK TENDERLOINS

Preparation Time
45 minutes

Cooking Time
7 hours and 15 minutes

Servings
4

INGREDIENTS

- 2 lb pork tenderloins
- 1 cup chicken broth
- ¼ cup lime juice
- 3 tsp chili powder
- 2 tsp garlic powder
- 1 tsp ginger powder
- ½ tsp sea salt

DIRECTIONS

1. Combine chili powder, garlic powder, ginger powder, and salt in a bowl. Rub the spice mixture all over the pork and place it in the Slow Cooker. Pour in the broth and lime juice around the pork. Cover with the lid and cook for 7 hours on low.
2. Remove the pork from the Slow Cooker and let rest for 5 minutes. Slice the pork against the grain into medallions before serving.

Nutritions: Calories: 182; Fat: 9 g; Saturated fat: 2 g; Protein: 24 g; Total carbs: 1 g; Sodium: 305 mg; Cholesterol: 74 mg

70. GARLIC TURKEY SKEWERS

Preparation Time
10 minutes

Cooking Time
15 minutes

Servings
4

INGREDIENTS

- 1 lb boneless, skinless turkey breasts, cut into cubes
- 1 lemon, juiced
- 2 tbsp avocado oil
- 2 tbsp garlic, crushed
- 1 tsp dried thyme
- 1 tsp dried oregano
- ½ tsp fine sea salt
- ¼ tsp ground black pepper

DIRECTIONS

1. Combine the turkey cubes, lemon juice, avocado oil, crushed garlic, dried thyme, dried oregano, fine sea salt, and ground black pepper in a large mixing bowl. Mix until well coated, and allow to rest for 30 minutes.
2. Spear the turkey cubes onto 8 skewers.
3. Heat a nonstick frying pan over medium-high heat.
4. Place the skewers in the pan, and cook for 5-7 minutes. Flip and cook for 5-8 minutes, or until fully cooked and browned. Remove from the heat, and serve.

Nutritions: Calories: 205; Total fat: 10 g; Saturated fat: 2 g; Sodium: 343 mg; Total carbs: 2 g; Fiber: 0 g; Protein: 26 g

71. ALMOND BUTTER CHICKEN

Preparation Time
10 minutes

Cooking Time
5 minutes

Servings
2

INGREDIENTS

- 2 tsp olive oil
- 1 tbsp garlic, crushed, divided
- ½ cup brown onion, finely chopped
- 8 oz lean ground chicken
- 1 tsp ginger, grated
- 3 tbsp unsalted almond butter
- 4 tbsp water
- 6 large iceberg lettuce leaves

DIRECTIONS

1. Heat the olive oil in an iron pan over medium heat. Add half of the crushed garlic and the chopped onion, and cook until translucent for 1-2 minutes.
2. Add the ground chicken, break it up with a fork, and cook for 5 minutes, until golden and cooked through.
3. Add together the grated ginger, remaining crushed garlic, almond butter, and water in a glass bowl, and mix to combine. Add the almond butter mixture to the chicken mixture, and cook for 1 minute until the flavors have combined.
4. Divide the chicken mixture into the iceberg lettuce cups and serve.

Nutritions: Calories: 414; Total fat: 21 g; Saturated fat: 4 g; Cholesterol: 90 mg; Sodium: 211 mg; Total carbs: 17 g; Net carbs: 7 g; Fiber: 4 g; Protein: 32 g

72. BALSAMIC BERRY CHICKEN

Preparation Time: 10 minutes
Cooking Time: 30 minutes
Servings: 2

INGREDIENTS

- Aluminum foil
- ½ cup blueberries
- 2 tbsp pine nuts
- ¼ cup basil, finely chopped
- 2 tbsp balsamic vinegar
- ¼ tsp ground black pepper
- 2 (4 oz) chicken breasts, butterflied

DIRECTIONS

1. Heat the oven to 375°F, gas mark 5. Line a medium-sized baking dish with aluminum foil.
2. Add together the blueberries, pine nuts, chopped basil, balsamic vinegar, and ground black pepper in a medium-sized mixing bowl. Mix until well combined.
3. Place the chicken pieces in the pan, and pour the blueberry mixture on top.
4. Bake for 20–30 minutes, or until the juices are caramelized, and the inside of the chicken is fully cooked.
5. Serve warm with a side dish of your choice.

Tip: To butterfly a chicken breast, cut the breast halfway through, horizontally.

Substitution tip: swap the blueberries for any berry of your choice.

Nutritions: Calories: 212; Total fat: 7 g; Saturated fat: 1 g; Cholesterol: 80 mg; Sodium: 58 mg; Total carbs: 11 g; Net carbs: 7 g; Fiber: 2 g; Protein: 27 g

73. SPICY TROUT SHEET PAN DINNER

Preparation Time
5 minutes

Cooking Time
20 minutes

Servings
5

INGREDIENTS

- 3 tbsp minced garlic, divided
- 2 tbsp chili powder, divided
- 2 tbsp olive oil, divided
- Sea salt to taste
- 1 lb rainbow trout fillets
- 2 zucchinis, sliced into rounds

DIRECTIONS

1. Preheat the oven to 425°F. Line a baking sheet with parchment paper.
2. In a medium bowl, mix 2 tbsp garlic, 1 tbsp chili powder, 1 tbsp olive oil, and a pinch of salt. Generously coat both sides of the trout fillets with the garlic mixture and place them on one half of the baking sheet.
3. In another medium bowl, mix the remaining garlic, chili powder, olive oil, and another pinch of salt. Add the zucchini to the bowl and stir to combine.
4. Bake the fish for 20 minutes until slightly browned on the edges. Add the zucchini to the empty side of the baking sheet halfway through the cooking time. Enjoy immediately.

Substitution tip: If the chili powder is too spicy for your liking, use lime juice instead.

Storage tip: Store any leftovers in an airtight container in the refrigerator for up to 5 days.

Nutritions: Calories: 186; Total fat: 9 g; Saturated fat: 2 g; Trans fat: 0 g; Protein: 20 g; Total carbohydrates: 6 g; Fiber: 2 g; Sodium: 158 mg; Potassium: 724 mg

74. MAPLE-GARLIC SALMON AND CAULIFLOWER SHEET PAN DINNER

Preparation Time
5 minutes + 30 minutes to marinate

Cooking Time
20 minutes

Servings
5

INGREDIENTS

- 1 lb salmon fillet
- 3 tbsp minced garlic, divided
- 2 tbsp olive oil, divided
- 2 tbsp low-sodium soy sauce
- Freshly ground black pepper
- 2 ½ cup bite-size cauliflower florets
- A pinch of sea salt
- 1 ½ tbsp maple syrup

DIRECTIONS

1. Place the salmon, 2 tbsp garlic, 1 tbsp oil, soy sauce, and pepper in a resealable plastic bag and place the bag in the refrigerator. Let the fish marinate for 30 minutes or overnight.
2. Preheat the oven to 425°F. Line a baking sheet with parchment paper.
3. In a medium bowl, toss the cauliflower with the remaining olive oil, garlic, more pepper, and a pinch of salt, and place it on half of the prepared baking sheet.
4. Place the marinated salmon on the other half of the sheet and bake for 20 minutes until the fish is slightly golden brown on the edges and just cooked through. Transfer the fish from the baking sheet to a plate and loosely cover it with foil to keep it warm. Flip the cauliflower and bake for 10 minutes more, until soft.
5. Drizzle the maple syrup over the salmon and serve with the cauliflower.

Tip: When buying fresh salmon, look for fillets that appear moist and bright in color, which indicates they are fresh.

Storage tip: Store in an airtight container in the refrigerator for up to 5 days.

Nutritions: Calories: 216; Total fat: 11 g; Saturated fat: 2 g; Trans fat: 0 g; Protein: 20 g; Total carbohydrates: 9 g; Fiber: 1 g; Sodium: 293 mg; Potassium: 658 mg

75. SALMON PATTIES

Preparation Time
20 minutes

Cooking Time
40 minutes

Servings
5

INGREDIENTS

- ¼ cup quinoa, rinsed
- ½ cup water
- 2 (7 ½ oz) cans of low-sodium deboned salmon, packed in water
- 1 tbsp mustard
- 1 tsp Old Bay seasoning
- 2 large eggs
- Olive oil

DIRECTIONS

1. In a medium saucepan over high heat, combine the quinoa and water and bring to a boil. Reduce the heat to low, and simmer until the liquid is absorbed, for about 20 minutes. Remove from the heat, fluff with a fork, and let cool.
2. Preheat the oven to 400°F. Line a baking sheet with parchment paper.
3. In a large bowl, mix the salmon, mustard, and seasoning until well combined.
4. Add the quinoa and eggs and combine well, then shape the mixture into 5 patties.
5. Place the patties on the prepared baking sheet and bake for 20 minutes, until they are slightly brown on the edges. Serve hot.

Substitution tip: Add ¼ cup Fresh Lime Salsa instead of Old Bay seasoning if you'd like to add some veggies and fresh citrus.

Storage tip: Freeze the patties in a sealed container for up to 2-3 months.

Nutritions: Calories: 202; Total fat: 10 g; Saturated fat: 2 g; Trans fat: 0 g; Protein: 23 g; Total carbohydrates: 6 g; Fiber: 1 g; Sodium: 480 mg; Potassium: 310 mg

76. SWEET SALAD DRESSING CHICKEN AND CARROT SHEET PAN DINNER

Preparation Time
5 minutes + 30 minutes to marinate

Cooking Time
25 minutes

Servings
5

INGREDIENTS

- 1 lb boneless, skinless chicken thighs
- ½ cup Sweet Salad dressing
- 2 ½ cup carrots, cut into thin matchsticks
- 1 ½ tbsp olive oil
- 1 tbsp minced garlic
- Sea salt to taste
- Freshly ground black pepper to taste

DIRECTIONS

1. Place the chicken and Sweet Salad dressing in a resealable plastic bag and marinate for 30 minutes or overnight in the refrigerator.
2. Preheat the oven to 425°F. Line a baking sheet with parchment.
3. In a medium bowl, toss the carrots with olive oil and garlic, season with salt and pepper, and set aside.
4. Place the chicken on half of the prepared baking sheet and bake for 25 minutes, or until it reaches an internal temperature of 165°F.
5. After 5 minutes, add the carrots to the other side of the baking sheet and bake them with the chicken for the remaining 20 minutes, flipping the carrots halfway through. Enjoy immediately.

Variation tip: Drizzle 1 tbsp honey onto the carrots before you bake them, to match the chicken's sweet flavor.

Storage tip: Store any leftovers in an airtight container in the refrigerator for up to 5 days.

Nutritions: Calories: 213; Total fat: 8 g; Saturated fat: 2 g; Trans fat: 0 g; Protein: 19 g; Total carbohydrates: 17 g; Fiber: 2 g; Sodium: 298 mg; Potassium: 553 mg

77. CHICKEN, MUSHROOM, AND BELL PEPPER SKEWERS

Preparation Time
10 minutes

Cooking Time
17 minutes

Servings
4

INGREDIENTS

- 1 lb skinless, boneless chicken breast, cut into 1-inch cubes
- ⅓ cup Oregano-Thyme sauce
- 2 bell peppers, cut into 1-inch chunks
- 24 whole white mushrooms
- 1 tbsp minced garlic
- 1 ½ tbsp olive oil
- Sea salt to taste

DIRECTIONS

1. Preheat the oven to 450°F. Line a baking sheet with parchment paper.
2. In a medium bowl, toss the chicken breast with the Oregano-Thyme sauce.
3. In another medium bowl, toss the peppers and mushrooms with garlic, olive oil, and a pinch of salt.
4. Thread the chicken, peppers, and mushrooms onto 8 wooden or metal skewers. (If using wooden skewers, be sure to soak them for 30 minutes beforehand.)
5. Place the skewers on the prepared baking sheet and bake for about 17 minutes, until the chicken edges are slightly brown and it is cooked to an internal temperature of 165°F. Serve immediately.

Cooking tip: Make sure to keep an eye on the chicken. Overbaking can make it dry and stringy.

Storage tip: Store in an airtight container in the refrigerator for up to 5 days.

Nutritions: Calories: 191; Total fat: 7 g; Saturated fat: 1 g; Trans fat: 0 g; Protein: 24 g; Total carbohydrates: 8 g; Fiber: 2 g; Sodium: 313 mg; Potassium: 685 mg

78. CHICKEN CURRY

Preparation Time
5 minutes

Cooking Time
15 minutes

Servings
5

INGREDIENTS

- 1 tbsp olive oil
- 1 lb boneless, skinless chicken thighs, thinly sliced
- 1 tbsp minced garlic
- 1 white onion, diced
- 2 tbsp curry powder
- ½ cup fat-free plain Greek yogurt
- A pinch of sea salt

DIRECTIONS

1. In a large skillet over medium heat, heat the olive oil and cook the chicken and garlic until the chicken is cooked through, for about 10 minutes.
2. Add the onion and cook until it is translucent, for about 5 minutes.
3. Add the curry powder and stir for 1-2 minutes until it is fragrant.
4. Remove the skillet from the heat, stir in the yogurt, and season with a pinch of salt. Serve immediately.

Serving tip: Add some chopped cilantro on top to add color and another burst of flavor.

Storage tip: Store any leftovers in a sealed container for up to 5 days in the refrigerator.

Nutritions: Calories: 160; Total fat: 7 g; Saturated fat: 1 g; Trans fat: 0 g; Protein: 20 g; Total carbohydrates: 4 g; Fiber: 2 g; Sodium: 124 mg; Potassium: 304 mg

79. LEMON CHICKEN AND ASPARAGUS

Preparation Time
10 minutes + 30 minutes to marinate

Cooking Time
20 minutes

Servings
5

INGREDIENTS

- 1 lb boneless, skinless chicken thighs, cut into 1-inch pieces
- ½ cup Lemon-Garlic sauce
- 2 ½ cup (about 1 lb) chopped asparagus
- 1 tbsp minced garlic
- 1 ½ tbsp olive oil
- Sea salt to taste
- Freshly ground black pepper to taste

DIRECTIONS

1. Place the chicken and Lemon-Garlic sauce in a resealable plastic bag and marinate in the refrigerator for 30 minutes or overnight.
2. In a medium bowl, toss the asparagus with the garlic and olive oil, and season with salt and pepper.
3. In a large skillet over high heat, sauté the chicken until cooked through and browned, about 15 minutes. Transfer the chicken with a slotted spoon to a plate and set aside.
4. Add the asparagus to the skillet and sauté until tender-crisp, about 5 minutes. Enjoy immediately.

Substitution tip: Instead of asparagus, use zucchini as the pairing vegetable.

Storage tip: Store any leftovers in a sealed container in the refrigerator for up to 5 days.

Nutritions: Calories: 221; Total fat: 13 g; Saturated fat: 3 g; Trans fat: 0 g; Protein: 20 g; Total carbohydrates: 6 g; Fiber: 2 g; Sodium: 352 mg; Potassium: 437 mg

80. TURKEY QUINOA CASSEROLE

Preparation Time
10 minutes

Cooking Time
30 minutes

Servings
5

INGREDIENTS

- 1 cup quinoa, rinsed
- 2 cup water
- 1 tbsp olive oil
- 1 lb lean ground turkey
- ⅓ cup Spicy Honey sauce
- 1 red bell pepper, diced
- 1 (19 oz) can of low-sodium corn, drained

DIRECTIONS

1. In a medium saucepan over high heat, combine the quinoa and water and bring to a boil. Reduce the heat to low, and simmer until the liquid is absorbed, for about 20 minutes. Remove from the heat, fluff with a fork, and let cool.
2. Preheat the oven to 375°F.
3. In a large skillet over medium-high heat, heat the olive oil and cook the ground turkey until browned, about 10 minutes.
4. Add the Spicy Honey sauce, the cooked quinoa, the bell pepper, and the corn, and stir to mix well.
5. Spread the turkey-quinoa mixture in a 9-inch square casserole dish and bake until the top edges are slightly brown, for about 10 minutes. Enjoy immediately.

Serving tip: Add some freshly minced cilantro and cubed avocado on top for a burst of freshness.

Storage tip: Freeze this casserole in a sealed container for up to 2–3 months.

Nutritions: Calories: 431; Total fat: 20 g; Saturated fat: 3 g; Trans fat: 0 g; Protein: 24 g; Total carbohydrates: 43 g; Fiber: 6 g; Sodium: 502 mg; Potassium: 597 mg

81. SHEET PAN HONEY-SOY BEEF BROCCOLI

Preparation Time
10 minutes + 30 minutes to marinate

Cooking Time
15 minutes

Servings
5

INGREDIENTS

- 1 lb lean beef, thinly sliced
- ⅓ cup Honey-Garlic sauce
- 2 ½ cup broccoli florets
- 1 ½ tbsp olive oil
- 1 tbsp minced garlic
- A pinch of sea salt

DIRECTIONS

1. Place the beef and the Honey-Garlic sauce in a resealable plastic bag, and marinate in the refrigerator for 30 minutes or overnight.
2. Preheat the oven to 450°F. Line a baking sheet with parchment paper.
3. In a medium bowl, toss the broccoli with olive oil, garlic, and a pinch of salt.
4. Spread the beef on half of the prepared sheet pan and the broccoli on the other half.
5. Bake for 15 minutes until the beef is slightly crisp. Enjoy immediately.

Variation tip: Sprinkle on some red pepper flakes for an extra kick.

Storage tip: Store any leftovers in a sealed container for up to 5 days in the refrigerator.

Nutritions: Calories: 207; Total fat: 10 g; Saturated fat: 2 g; Trans fat: 0 g; Protein: 22 g; Total carbohydrates: 7 g; Fiber: 1 g; Sodium: 265 mg; Potassium: 392 mg

82. HEART-HEALTHY MEATLOAF

Preparation Time
5 minutes

Cooking Time
55 minutes

Servings
5

INGREDIENTS

- 1 lb lean ground beef
- 1 cup whole-grain breadcrumbs
- ¾ cup Tasty Tomato sauce, divided
- 1 large egg
- ½ white onion, diced

DIRECTIONS

1. Preheat the oven to 350°F. Line a baking sheet with parchment paper.
2. In a large bowl, combine the beef, breadcrumbs, ½ cup Tasty Tomato sauce, egg, and onion. Shape the ground beef mixture into a loaf and place it on the prepared baking sheet.
3. Spread the remaining Tasty Tomato sauce on top of the meatloaf and bake for 55 minutes, or until the internal temperature reaches 160°F. Serve immediately.

Cooking tip: Bake 4 mini versions in muffin tins to cut the cooking time to about 30 minutes.

Storage tip: Store any leftovers in a sealed container in the refrigerator for up to 5 days.

Nutritions: Calories: 269; Total fat: 7 g; Saturated fat: 3 g; Trans fat: 0 g; Protein: 24 g; Total carbohydrates: 27 g; Fiber: 1 g; Sodium: 228 mg; Potassium: 463 mg

83. EASY LEAN BEEF WITH CARROTS AND POTATOES

Preparation Time
10 minutes

Cooking Time
15 minutes

Servings
4

INGREDIENTS

- 2 tbsp olive oil
- 1 cup diced carrots
- 1 red onion, diced
- 2 red potatoes, skins on and diced
- 1 lb lean ground beef
- ⅓ cup Oregano-Thyme sauce

DIRECTIONS

1. In a large skillet over medium heat, heat the olive oil, carrots, onion, and potatoes. Toss with tongs and cook for 5 minutes, until slightly aromatic.
2. Push the mixture to one side of the skillet and add the ground beef to the other side.
3. Pour the Oregano-Thyme sauce over the top of the beef and toss with tongs.
4. Increase the heat to high and cook the beef, stirring frequently, for 10 minutes, until it's no longer pink.
5. Mix the potato, carrot, and onion mixture with the cooked ground beef and serve.

Storage tip: Store any leftovers in an airtight container in the refrigerator for up to 5 days.

Nutritions: Calories: 315; Total fat: 13 g; Saturated fat: 3 g; Trans fat: 0 g; Protein: 27 g; Total carbohydrates: 24 g; Fiber: 3 g; Sodium: 349 mg; Potassium: 1,025 mg

84. SPICY HONEY CHICKEN AND EGGPLANT

Preparation Time
10 minutes + 30 minutes to marinate

Cooking Time
30 minutes

Servings
5

INGREDIENTS

- 1 lb boneless, skinless chicken thighs
- ⅓ cup Spicy Honey sauce
- 2 eggplants, cut into ¼-inch-thick slices
- 2 tbsp minced garlic
- Sea salt to taste
- Freshly ground black pepper to taste

DIRECTIONS

1. Place the chicken and the Spicy Honey sauce in a resealable plastic bag, and marinate in the refrigerator for 30 minutes or overnight.
2. Preheat the oven to 400°F. Line a baking sheet with parchment paper.
3. Place the eggplant slices on half of the prepared baking sheet, sprinkle them with the garlic, and season them with salt and pepper.
4. Spread out the chicken on the other half of the baking sheet.
5. Cook until the eggplant is caramelized and the chicken reaches an internal temperature of 165°F, about 25–30 minutes. Serve immediately.

Storage tip: Store any leftovers in a sealed container in the refrigerator for up to 5 days.

Nutritions: Calories: 248; Total fat: 10 g; Saturated fat: 1 g; Trans fat: 0 g; Protein: 20 g; Total carbohydrates: 21 g; Fiber: 8 g; Sodium: 370 mg; Potassium: 741 mg

85. TURKEY MEATBALLS

Preparation Time
5 minutes

Cooking Time
15 minutes

Servings
20

INGREDIENTS

- 1 lb lean ground turkey
- 1 ½ cup Spinach and Walnut Pesto
- ½ cup whole-grain breadcrumbs
- 1 large egg
- ½ white onion, finely diced

DIRECTIONS

1. Preheat the oven to 375°F. Line a baking sheet with parchment paper.
2. In a medium bowl, mix the turkey, Spinach and Walnut Pesto, breadcrumbs, egg, and onion until well combined.
3. With your hands, form the mixture into about 20 (1 ½-inch) meatballs.
4. Place the meatballs on the prepared baking sheet and bake for 15 minutes, or until the internal temperature reaches 165°F. Serve immediately.

Serving tip: Add 4 cups of diced, cooked carrots and celery to these meatballs for an extra serving of vegetables.

Storage tip: Store the meatballs in an airtight container in the refrigerator for up to 5 days or in the freezer for up to 3 months.

Nutritions: Calories: 440; Total fat: 37 g; Saturated fat: 6 g; Trans fat: 0 g; Protein: 17 g; Total carbohydrates: 10 g; Fiber: 2 g; Sodium: 373 mg; Potassium: 336 mg

86. GREEK PIZZA

Preparation Time
15 minutes

Cooking Time
25 minutes

Servings
5

INGREDIENTS

- 1 ½ cup whole wheat or whole-grain self-rising flour + more for dusting
- 1 cup low-fat plain Greek yogurt
- 1 ½ cup Spinach and Walnut Pesto
- 1 tomato, thinly sliced
- ½ cup thinly sliced white mushrooms

DIRECTIONS

1. Preheat the oven to 350°F. Line a baking sheet with parchment paper.
2. In a medium bowl, place the flour. Mix in the yogurt ¼ cup at a time until the dough is smooth. Knead it into a ball.
3. Sprinkle 1 or 2 tbsp flour onto a cutting board or hard, clean surface, and form the dough ball into a 12-inch circle.
4. Transfer the dough to the baking sheet and spread it evenly with the Spinach and Walnut Pesto.
5. Arrange the tomato and mushrooms on top of the sauce.
6. Bake the pizza for 25 minutes, until the crust is golden brown. Enjoy immediately.

Cooking tip: Make your own self-rising flour by mixing 1 ½ cup flour, 2 tsp baking powder, and ¼ tsp salt.

Nutritions: Calories: 433; Total fat: 31 g; Saturated fat: 5 g; Trans fat: 0 g; Protein: 10 g; Total carbohydrates: 33 g; Fiber: 5 g; Sodium: 279 mg; Potassium: 443 mg

87. SPINACH, WALNUT, AND BLACK BEAN BURGERS

Preparation Time
10 minutes

Cooking Time
20 minutes

Servings
6

INGREDIENTS

- 1 tbsp olive oil
- 1 white onion, diced
- 1 cup Spinach and Walnut Pesto
- 2 (19 oz) cans of low-sodium black beans, drained and rinsed
- 2 large eggs
- ½ cup whole wheat or whole-grain breadcrumbs

DIRECTIONS

1. Preheat the oven to 375°F. Line a baking sheet with parchment paper.
2. In a medium skillet, heat the olive oil over high heat and sauté the onion until translucent, about 3 minutes.
3. Put the onion, the Spinach and Walnut Pesto, beans, eggs, and breadcrumbs into a blender or food processor and pulse until combined.
4. Using a ½-cup scoop, form 6 patties and place them on the prepared baking sheet.
5. Bake the patties in the oven for 20 minutes. Enjoy immediately.

Cooking tip: Dry off the black beans with a paper towel before blending to prevent mushy burgers.

Storage tip: Store the burgers in an airtight container in the freezer for up to 3 months.

Nutritions: Calories: 383; Total fat: 24 g; Saturated fat: 4 g; Trans fat: 0 g; Protein: 12 g; Total carbohydrates: 32 g; Fiber: 9 g; Sodium: 253 mg; Potassium: 461 mg

88. LOADED VEGGIE-STUFFED PEPPERS

Preparation Time: 15 minutes
Cooking Time: 1 hour
Servings: 6

INGREDIENTS

- ½ cup brown rice, rinsed
- 1 cup water
- 1 (19 oz) can of low-sodium black beans, drained and rinsed
- 1 (12 oz) can of low-sodium corn, drained
- 1 cup Fresh Lime Salsa
- 6 orange bell peppers, halved top to bottom and seeded
- Olive oil

DIRECTIONS

1. In a medium saucepan over high heat, combine the rice and water and bring to a boil. Cover, reduce the heat to low, and simmer until the liquid is absorbed, for about 30 minutes. Remove from the heat, fluff with a fork, and let cool.
2. Preheat the oven to 375°F. Line a baking sheet with parchment paper.
3. In a medium bowl, combine the rice, black beans, corn, and Fresh Lime Salsa.
4. Lightly brush the outside of the bell pepper halves with oil.
5. Evenly distribute the bean mixture among the bell pepper halves. Place the peppers on the prepared baking sheet and cover them with aluminum foil.
6. Bake the stuffed peppers for 20 minutes, remove the foil, and bake for another 10 minutes until fragrant. Enjoy immediately.

Substitution tip: Substitute the brown rice with cooked quinoa for a boost of protein.

Storage tip: Store the stuffed peppers in an airtight container in the refrigerator for up to 2 days.

Nutritions: Calories: 279; Total fat: 3 g; Saturated fat: 0 g; Trans fat: 0 g; Protein: 11 g; Total carbohydrates: 56 g; Fiber: 10 g; Sodium: 122 mg; Potassium: 1,201 mg

89. CHICKEN WITH BLACK OLIVES, CAPERS, AND RICE OIL

Preparation Time
15 minutes

Cooking Time
35 minutes

Servings
4

INGREDIENTS

- 17 oz chicken breast
- 4 tbsp pitted black olives
- 3 tbsp capers
- 3 tbsp rice oil
- Flour to taste
- Salt to taste
- Black pepper to taste

DIRECTIONS

1. For a better yield in seasoning, it is preferable to chop the olives into smaller pieces; then, wash the capers under running water to remove the salt from them.
2. At this point, flour the chicken breast lightly, then place it in a baking pan (cover the bottom of the pan with a sheet of baking paper).
3. Then, cover the chicken breast with the olives and capers, adding a little salt and pepper seasoning; bake at 180°C for 15 minutes.
4. When cooked, season the chicken by distributing the indicated amount of rice oil; portion and serve.

Nutritions: Calories: 184; Total fat: 12 g; Saturated fat: 2.8 g; Sodium: 166 mg; Total carbs: 3 g; Sugar: 2 g; Protein: 12 g

90. BASIL PESTO CHICKEN

Preparation Time
10 minutes

Cooking Time
15 minutes

Servings
4

INGREDIENTS

- 8 oz uncooked rotini pasta
- 1 lb asparagus, woody ends removed and cut into bite-size pieces
- 1 tbsp coconut oil
- 2 medium Roma tomatoes, chopped
- ½ cup basil pesto
- 12 oz boneless, cut into bite-size cubes, skinless chicken breasts
- ¼ cup Parmesan cheese, grated

DIRECTIONS

1. Follow the package directions for cooking the rotini pasta or al dente. Scoop out ½ cup the cooking water, and keep it aside. Add the asparagus pieces to the pasta when it reaches the remaining 4 minutes. Allow boiling.
2. Heat the coconut oil over medium-high heat in a large, heavy-bottom pan. Fry the cubed chicken breasts for 5–10 minutes or until cooked through. Stir in the chopped tomatoes, and remove the pan from the heat.
3. Drain the pasta and asparagus in a colander, and return them to the stockpot.
4. Toss the pasta and asparagus with the basil pesto and ¼ cup the reserved cooking water. Add the cooked chicken mixture and more cooking water if needed.
5. Top with the grated Parmesan cheese, and serve hot.

Nutritions: Calories: 485; Total fat: 17 g; Saturated fat: 4 g; Cholesterol: 68 mg; Sodium: 201 mg; Total carbs: 50 g; Fiber: 5 g; Protein: 33 g

91. OLIVE TURKEY PATTIES

Preparation Time
10 minutes

Cooking Time
30 minutes

Servings
4

INGREDIENTS

- Aluminum foil
- 1 lb lean ground turkey
- ½ cup rolled oats
- ¼ cup sliced black olives, chopped
- ¼ cup white onion, finely chopped
- ¼ cup parsley, finely chopped
- 1 tbsp garlic, minced
- 6 whole-wheat hamburger buns
- 1 ripe avocado, peeled, pitted, and sliced
- 6 iceberg lettuce leaves
- 6 beefsteak tomato slices

DIRECTIONS

1. Preheat the broiler and set a baking sheet about 3 inches from the heat source. Line a baking sheet with aluminum foil.
2. In a large mixing bowl, add the ground turkey, rolled oats, chopped black olives, chopped onion, chopped parsley, and minced garlic. Mix well until combined. Shape into 6 equal patties.
3. Place the turkey patties on the baking sheet, and broil for 3–4 minutes on each side, or until the juices run clear.
4. Meanwhile, place the whole-wheat buns, sliced avocado, iceberg lettuce, and tomato slices on a serving platter. Allow people to assemble their burgers.

Nutritions: Calories: 366; Total fat: 15 g; Saturated fat: 3 g; Cholesterol: 52 mg; Sodium: 353 mg; Total carbs: 35 g; Fiber: 6 g; Protein: 24 g

92. BROCCOLI CHICKEN RICE

Preparation Time
15 minutes

Cooking Time
20 minutes

Servings
4

INGREDIENTS

- 1 lb boneless, skinless chicken breasts, halved lengthwise
- ½ tsp Italian seasoning
- ½ tsp sea salt
- ¼ tsp ground black pepper
- 2 tbsp avocado oil, divided
- 4 cup broccoli rice
- 1 (15 oz) can of artichoke hearts, drained
- ¼ cup capers

DIRECTIONS

1. Season the chicken with Italian seasoning, sea salt, and ground black pepper.
2. Warm 1 tbsp avocado oil in a large, heavy-bottom pan over medium-high heat.
3. Add the seasoned chicken breasts and cook for 3-5 minutes or until browned.
4. Flip and cook for 4-6 minutes, or until fully cooked. Transfer onto a cutting board and thinly slice the chicken.
5. Heat the last 1 tbsp avocado oil in the same pan. Add the broccoli rice, and cook for 5-8 minutes, frequently stirring, until tender.
6. Add the artichoke hearts and capers, and mix until fully incorporated. Remove from the heat.
7. Serve the broccoli rice and vegetables, and top with the sliced chicken breasts.

Tip: Broccoli rice is broccoli florets that are chopped into the size of rice grains.

Nutritions: Calories: 270; Total fat: 11 g; Saturated fat: 2 g; Sodium: 481 mg; Total carbs: 14 g; Fiber: 6 g; Protein: 30 g

93. CHICKEN MEATBALLS

Preparation Time: 10 minutes
Cooking Time: 15 minutes
Servings: 4

INGREDIENTS

- Aluminum foil
- 1 lb lean ground chicken
- 1 cup courgettes, shredded
- ½ cup red onion, finely diced
- 3 tbsp black olives, minced
- 1 tbsp Mediterranean Seasoning Rub Blend
- 1 cup grape tomatoes

DIRECTIONS

1. Heat the oven to broil, and set an oven rack 6 inches from the broiler. Line a baking sheet with aluminum foil.
2. In a wide-sized mixing bowl, combine the ground chicken, shredded courgettes, diced onion, minced black olives, and Mediterranean seasoning blend. Allow marinating for 10 minutes.
3. Mold each spoon of the chicken mixture into a meatball to make 8 total, and place them on the baking sheet with the grape tomatoes.
4. Broil for 6-12 minutes, until golden brown and fully cooked. The tomatoes should be blistered.
5. Serve with your side of choice.

Nutritions: Calories: 160; Total fat: 5 g; Saturated fat: 1 g; Cholesterol: 90 mg; Sodium: 107 mg; Total carbs: 6 g; Net carbs: 3 g; Fiber: 2 g; Protein: 24 g

94. PARMESAN PORK CHOPS

Preparation Time 15 minutes

Cooking Time 25 minutes

Servings 4

INGREDIENTS

- 2 tbsp avocado oil
- 4 thick pork chops, fat trimmed
- ½ red onion, chopped
- 1 ½ cup couscous
- 2 ½ cup water
- ½ cup sun-dried tomatoes, chopped
- 3 cup kale, finely chopped
- ¼ cup Parmesan cheese, grated

DIRECTIONS

1. Warm the avocado oil in an iron pot over high heat.
2. Add the pork chops, and fry for 1 ½ minute on each side, until browned. Transfer to a plate.
3. Reduce the heat to medium. Add the onion and cook it for 6 minutes or until it has softened.
4. Add the couscous, and cook for 1–2 minutes, until browned.
5. Put in the water and scrape the bottom of the pan to deglaze it.
6. Add the chopped sun-dried tomatoes, and allow to simmer for 5 minutes.
7. Add the pork chunks back to the pot, cover, and turn the heat down to low. Cook for 6–8 minutes, or until the chops are fully cooked and the couscous is tender.
8. Remove the iron pot from the heat and add the grated Parmesan and chopped greens, stirring until the kale is wilted. Serve warm.

Tip: If the couscous starts to dry out, add 2 tbsp water at a time to keep it moist.

Nutritions: Calories: 484; Total fat: 18 g; Saturated fat: 4 g; Sodium: 103 mg; Total carbs: 48 g; Fiber: 4 g; Protein: 32 g

95. CANNELLINI BEAN LETTUCE WRAPS

Preparation Time
15 minutes

Cooking Time
10 minutes

Servings
4

INGREDIENTS

- 1 tbsp extra-virgin olive oil
- ½ cup diced red onion (about ¼ onion)
- ¾ cup chopped fresh tomatoes (about 1 medium tomato)
- ¼ tsp freshly ground black pepper
- 1 (15 oz) can of cannellini or great northern beans, drained and rinsed
- ¼ cup finely chopped fresh curly parsley
- ½ cup Lemony Garlic Hummus or ½ cup prepared hummus
- 8 Romaine lettuce leaves

DIRECTIONS

1. In a large skillet over medium heat, heat the oil. Add the onion and cook for 3 minutes, stirring occasionally.
2. Add the tomatoes and pepper and cook for 3 more minutes, stirring occasionally. Add the beans and cook for 3 more minutes, stirring occasionally. Remove from the heat, and mix in the parsley.
3. Spread 1 tbsp hummus over each lettuce leaf. Evenly spread the warm bean mixture down the center of each leaf.
4. Fold one side of the lettuce leaf over the filling lengthwise, then fold over the other side to make a wrap and serve.

Nutritions: Calories: 211; Fat: 8 g; Carbohydrates: 28 g; Protein: 10 g

96. ISRAELI EGGPLANT, CHICKPEA, AND MINT SAUTÉ

Preparation Time
5 minutes

Cooking Time
20 minutes

Servings
6

INGREDIENTS

- Nonstick cooking spray
- 1 medium globe eggplant (about 1 lb), stem removed
- 1 tbsp extra-virgin olive oil
- 2 tbsp freshly squeezed lemon juice (from about 1 small lemon)
- 2 tbsp balsamic vinegar
- 1 tsp ground cumin
- ¼ tsp kosher or sea salt
- 1 (15 oz) can of chickpeas, drained and rinsed
- 1 cup sliced sweet onion (about ½ medium Walla Walla or Vidalia onion)
- ¼ cup loosely packed chopped or torn mint leaves
- 1 tbsp sesame seeds, toasted if desired
- 1 garlic clove, finely minced (about ½ tsp)

DIRECTIONS

1. Place one oven rack about 4 inches below the broiler element. Turn the broiler to the highest setting to preheat. Spray a large, rimmed baking sheet with nonstick cooking spray.
2. On a cutting board, cut the eggplant lengthwise into 4 slabs (each piece should be about ½–⅛-inch thick). Place the eggplant slabs on the prepared baking sheet. Set aside.
3. In a small bowl, whisk together the oil, lemon juice, vinegar, cumin, and salt. Brush or drizzle 2 tbsp the lemon dressing over both sides of the eggplant slabs. Reserve the remaining dressing.
4. Broil the eggplant directly under the heating element for 4 minutes, flip them, then broil for another 4 minutes, until golden brown.
5. While the eggplant is broiling, in a serving bowl, combine the chickpeas, onion, mint, sesame seeds, and garlic. Add the reserved dressing, and gently mix to incorporate all the ingredients.
6. When the eggplant is done, using tongs, transfer the slabs from the baking sheet to a cooling rack and let them cool for 3 minutes.
7. When slightly cooled, place the eggplants on a cutting board and slice each slab crosswise into ½-inch strips.
8. Add the eggplant to the serving bowl with the onion mixture. Gently toss everything together, and serve warm or at room temperature.

Nutritions: Calories: 159; Fat: 4 g; Carbohydrates: 26 g; Protein: 6 g

97. MINESTRONE CHICKPEAS AND MACARONI CASSEROLE

Preparation Time
15 minutes

Cooking Time
7 hours and 25 minutes

Servings
5

INGREDIENTS

- 1 (15 oz/425 g) can of chickpeas, drained and rinsed
- 1 (28 oz/794 g) can of diced tomatoes, with the juice
- 1 (6 oz/170 g) can of no-salt-added tomato paste
- 3 medium carrots, sliced
- 3 garlic cloves, minced
- 1 medium yellow onion, chopped
- 1 cup low-sodium vegetable soup
- ½ tsp dried rosemary
- 1 tsp dried oregano
- 2 tsp maple syrup
- ½ tsp sea salt
- ¼ tsp ground black pepper
- ½ lb (227 g) of fresh green beans, trimmed and cut into bite-size pieces
- 1 cup macaroni pasta
- 2 oz (57 g) Parmesan cheese, grated

DIRECTIONS

1. Except for the green beans, pasta, and Parmesan cheese, combine all the ingredients in the Slow Cooker and stir to mix well. Put the Slow Cooker lid on and cook on low for 7 hours.
2. Fold in the pasta and green beans. Put the lid on and cook on high for 20 minutes or until the vegetable are soft and the pasta is al dente.
3. Pour the pasta into a large serving bowl and spread with Parmesan cheese before serving.

Nutritions: Calories: 349; Fat: 6.7 g; Protein: 16.5 g; Carbs: 59.9 g

98. SPICED SOUP WITH LENTILS AND LEGUMES

Preparation Time
15 minutes

Cooking Time
35 minutes

Servings
2

INGREDIENTS

- 2 tbsp extra-virgin olive oil
- 2 garlic cloves, minced
- 4 large celery stalks, diced
- 2 large onions, diced
- 6 cup water
- 1 tsp cumin
- ¾ tsp turmeric
- ½ tsp cinnamon
- ½ tsp fresh ginger, grated
- 1 cup dried lentils, rinsed and sorted
- 1 (16 oz) can of chickpeas (garbanzo beans), drained and rinsed
- 3 ripe tomatoes, cubed
- ½ lemon, juice
- ½ cup fresh cilantro or parsley, chopped
- Salt to taste

DIRECTIONS

1. Heat the olive oil and sauté the garlic, celery, and onion for 5 minutes in a large stockpot placed over medium heat.
2. Pour in the water. Add the spices and lentils. Cover the stockpot and simmer for 40 minutes until the lentils are tender.
3. Add the chickpeas and tomatoes. (Pour more water and additional spices, if desired.) Simmer for 15 minutes over low heat.
4. Pour in the lemon juice and stir the soup. Add the cilantro or parsley and salt to taste.

Nutritions: Calories: 123; Fat: 3 g; Dietary fiber: 5 g; Carbohydrates: 19 g; Protein: 5 g

99. BROWN RICE PILAF WITH GOLDEN RAISINS

Preparation Time
5 minutes

Cooking Time
15 minutes

Servings
6

INGREDIENTS

- 1 tbsp extra-virgin olive oil
- 1 cup chopped onion (about ½ medium onion)
- ½ cup shredded carrot (about 1 medium carrot)
- 1 tsp ground cumin
- ½ tsp ground cinnamon
- 2 cup instant brown rice
- 1 ¾ cup 100% orange juice
- ¼ cup water
- 1 cup golden raisins
- ½ cup shelled pistachios
- Chopped fresh chives (optional)

DIRECTIONS

1. In a medium saucepan over medium-high heat, heat the oil.
2. Add the onion and cook for 5 minutes, stirring frequently.
3. Add the carrot, cumin, and cinnamon, and cook for 1 minute, stirring frequently.
4. Stir in the rice, orange juice, and water.
5. Bring to a boil, cover, then lower the heat to medium-low.
6. Simmer for 7 minutes, or until the rice is cooked through and the liquid is absorbed.
7. Stir in the raisins, pistachios, and chives (if using) and serve.

Nutritions: Calories: 320; Fat: 7 g; Carbohydrates: 61 g; Protein: 6 g

100. RITZY VEGGIE CHILI

Preparation Time
15 minutes

Cooking Time
5 hours

Servings
4

INGREDIENTS

- 1 (28 oz/794 g) can of chopped tomatoes, with the juice
- 1 (15 oz/425 g) can of black beans, drained and rinsed
- 1 (15 oz/425 g) can of red beans, drained and rinsed
- 1 medium green bell pepper, chopped
- 1 yellow onion, chopped
- 1 tbsp onion powder
- 1 tsp paprika
- 1 tsp cayenne pepper
- 1 tsp garlic powder
- ½ tsp sea salt
- ½ tsp ground black pepper
- 1 tbsp olive oil
- 1 large Hass avocado, pitted, peeled, and chopped, for garnish

DIRECTIONS

1. Combine all the ingredients in the Slow Cooker, except for the avocado. Stir to mix well.
2. Put the Slow Cooker lid on and cook on high for 5 hours or until the vegetables are tender and the mixture has a thick consistency.
3. Pour the chili into a large serving bowl. Allow to cool for 30 minutes, then spread with chopped avocado and serve.

Nutritions: Calories: 633; Fat: 16.3 g; Protein: 31.7 g; Carbs: 97.0 g

DINNER

101. ROASTED SHRIMP AND VEGGIES

Preparation Time 10 minutes | **Cooking Time** 20 minutes | **Servings** 4

INGREDIENTS

- 1 cup sliced cremini mushrooms
- 2 medium chopped Yukon Gold potatoes, rinsed, unpeeled
- 2 cup broccoli florets
- 3 garlic cloves, sliced
- 1 cup sliced fresh green beans
- 1 cup cauliflower florets
- 2 tbsp fresh lemon juice
- 2 tbsp low-sodium vegetable broth
- 1 tsp olive oil
- 1 tsp dried thyme
- ½ tsp dried oregano
- A pinch of salt
- ⅛ tsp black pepper
- ½ lb medium shrimp, peeled and deveined

DIRECTIONS

1. Preheat the oven to 400°F.
2. In a large baking pan, combine the mushrooms, potatoes, broccoli, garlic, green beans, and cauliflower, and toss to coat.
3. In a small bowl, combine the lemon juice, broth, olive oil, thyme, oregano, salt, and pepper and mix well. Drizzle over the vegetables
4. Roast for 15 minutes, then stir.
5. Add the shrimp and distribute it evenly.
6. Roast for another 5 minutes or until the shrimp curl and turn pink. Serve immediately.

Nutritions: Calories: 192; Fat: 3 g (with 14% calories from fat); Saturated fat: 0 g; Monounsaturated fat: 1 g; Carbs: 29 g; Sodium: 116 mg; Dietary fiber: 5 g; Protein: 17 g; Cholesterol: 86 mg
- Vitamin A: 12% DV

Vitamin C: 138% DV; Sugar: 3 g

102. SHRIMP AND PINEAPPLE LETTUCE WRAPS

Preparation Time
15 minutes

Cooking Time
12 minutes

Servings
4

INGREDIENTS

- 2 tsp olive oil
- 2 jalapeño peppers, seeded and minced
- 6 scallions, chopped
- 2 yellow bell peppers, seeded and chopped
- 8 oz small shrimp, peeled and deveined
- 2 cup canned pineapple chunks, drained, reserving juice
- 2 tbsp fresh lime juice
- 1 avocado, peeled and cubed
- 1 large carrot, coarsely grated
- 8 romaine or Boston lettuce leaves, rinsed and dried

DIRECTIONS

1. In a medium saucepan, heat the olive oil over medium heat.
2. Add the jalapeño pepper and scallions and cook for 2 minutes, stirring constantly.
3. Add the bell pepper, and cook for 2 minutes.
4. Add the shrimp, and cook for 1 minute, stirring constantly.
5. Add the pineapple, 2 tbsp the reserved pineapple juice, and lime juice, and bring to a simmer. Simmer for 1 minute or until the shrimp curl and turn pink. Let the mixture cool for 5 minutes.
6. Serve the shrimp mixture with the cubed avocado and grated carrot, wrapped in the lettuce leaves.

Nutritions: Calories: 241; Fat: 9 g (with 33% calories from fat); Saturated fat: 2 g; Monounsaturated fat: 5 g; Carbs: 29 g; Sodium: 109 mg; Dietary fiber: 6 g; Protein: 6 g; Cholesterol: 109 mg
- Vitamin A: 96% DV

Vitamin C: 332% DV; Sugar: 16 g

103. GRILLED SCALLOPS WITH GREMOLATA

Preparation Time
15 minutes

Cooking Time
6 minutes

Servings
4

INGREDIENTS

- 2 scallions, cut into pieces
- ¾ cup packed fresh flat-leaf parsley
- ¼ cup packed fresh basil leaves
- 1 tsp lemon zest
- 3 tbsp fresh lemon juice
- 1 tbsp olive oil
- 20 sea scallops
- 2 tsp butter, melted
- A pinch of salt
- ⅛ tsp lemon pepper

DIRECTIONS

1. Prepare and preheat the grill to medium-high. Make sure the grill rack is clean.
2. Meanwhile, make the gremolata. In a blender or food processor, combine the scallions, parsley, basil, lemon zest, lemon juice, and olive oil. Blend or process until the herbs are finely chopped. Pour into a small bowl and set aside.
3. Put the scallops on a plate. If the scallops have a small tough muscle attached to them, remove and discard it. Brush the melted butter over the scallops. Sprinkle with salt and lemon pepper.
4. Place the scallops in a grill basket, if you have one. If not, place a sheet of heavy-duty foil on the grill, punch some holes in it, and arrange the scallops evenly across it.
5. Grill the scallops for 2-3 minutes per side, turning once, until opaque. Drizzle with the gremolata and serve.

Nutritions: Calories: 190; Fat: 7 g (with 33% calories from fat); Saturated fat: 2 g; Monounsaturated fat: 3 g; Carbs: 2 g; Sodium: 336 mg; Dietary fiber: 1 g; Protein: 28 g; Cholesterol: 68 mg
- Vitamin A: 27% DV

Vitamin C: 37% DV; Sugar: 1 g

104. HEALTHY PAELLA

Preparation Time 15 minutes

Cooking Time 15 minutes

Servings 4

INGREDIENTS

- 1 tbsp olive oil
- 1 onion, chopped
- 3 garlic cloves, minced
- 1 red bell pepper, seeded and chopped
- 2 ½ cup low-sodium vegetable broth
- 1 tomato, chopped
- 1 tsp smoked paprika
- 1 tsp dried thyme leaves
- ¼ tsp turmeric
- ⅛ tsp black pepper
- 1 cup whole-wheat orzo
- ½ lb halibut fillets, cut into 1-inch pieces
- 12 medium shrimp, peeled and deveined
- ¼ cup chopped fresh flat-leaf parsley

DIRECTIONS

1. In a large deep skillet, heat the olive oil over medium heat.
2. Add the onion, garlic, and red bell pepper, and cook, stirring, for 2 minutes.
3. Add the vegetable broth, tomato, paprika, thyme, turmeric, and black pepper, and bring to a simmer.
4. Stir in the orzo, making sure it is submerged in the liquid in the pan. Simmer for 5 minutes, stirring occasionally.
5. Add the halibut and stir. Simmer for 4 minutes.
6. Add the shrimp and stir. Simmer for 2–3 minutes or until the shrimp curl and turn pink and the pasta is cooked al dente.
7. Sprinkle with parsley and serve immediately.

Nutritions: Calories: 367; Fat: 7 g (with 17% calories from fat); Saturated fat: 1 g; Monounsaturated fat: 3 g; Carbs: 50 g; Sodium: 147 mg; Dietary fiber: 9 g; Protein: 25 g; Cholesterol: 50 mg
- Vitamin A: 38% DV

Vitamin C: 84% DV; Sugar: 5 g

105. VIETNAMESE FISH AND NOODLE BOWL

Preparation Time
15 minutes

Cooking Time
15 minutes

Servings
3

INGREDIENTS

- ¾ lb grouper fillets, cut into 1-inch pieces
- 1 tbsp cornstarch
- ⅛ tsp cayenne pepper
- 2 tsp fish sauce
- 1 tbsp rice wine vinegar
- 1 tsp sugar
- 2 tbsp fresh lemon juice
- 1 tsp olive oil
- ¼ cup minced daikon radish
- 3 garlic cloves, minced
- 4 oz whole-wheat spaghetti, broken in half
- 1 ½ cup low-sodium vegetable broth
- 2 tbsp chopped peanuts
- 2 tbsp minced fresh cilantro
- 2 tbsp minced fresh basil

DIRECTIONS

1. In a medium bowl, toss the grouper with the cornstarch and cayenne pepper and set aside.
2. In a small bowl, combine the fish sauce, rice wine vinegar, sugar, and lemon juice, and stir to mix well.
3. In a large skillet, heat the olive oil over medium heat. Add the daikon and garlic and cook for 1 minute, stirring constantly.
4. Add the fish to the skillet; sauté for 2–3 minutes, stirring frequently, until the fish browns lightly.
5. Remove the fish mixture to a large bowl and set aside.
6. Add the spaghetti and vegetable broth to the skillet, and stir. Bring to a simmer over high heat and cook for 7–8 minutes or until the pasta is al dente.
7. Return the fish and radish mixture to the skillet along with the fish sauce mixture, peanuts, cilantro, and basil. Toss for 1 minute, then serve immediately in bowls.

Nutritions: Calories: 324; Fat: 6 g (with 17% calories from fat); Saturated fat: 1 g; Monounsaturated fat: 3 g; Carbs: 38 g; Sodium: 439 mg; Dietary fiber: 1 g; Protein: 30 g; Cholesterol: 46 mg
- Vitamin A: 7% DV

Vitamin C: 12% DV; Sugar: 3 g

106. COD SATAY

Preparation Time: 15 minutes
Cooking Time: 15 minutes
Servings: 4

INGREDIENTS

- 2 tsp olive oil, divided
- 1 small onion, diced
- 2 garlic cloves, minced
- ⅓ cup low-fat coconut milk
- 1 tomato, chopped
- 2 tbsp low-fat peanut butter
- 1 tbsp packed brown sugar
- ⅓ cup low-sodium vegetable broth
- 2 tsp low-sodium soy sauce
- ⅛ tsp ground ginger
- A pinch of red pepper flakes
- 4 (6 oz) cod fillets
- ⅛ tsp white pepper

DIRECTIONS

1. In a small saucepan, heat 1 tsp the olive oil over medium heat.
2. Add the onion and garlic, and cook, stirring frequently for 3 minutes.
3. Add the coconut milk, tomato, peanut butter, brown sugar, broth, soy sauce, ginger, and red pepper flakes, and bring to a simmer, stirring with a whisk until the sauce combines. Simmer for 2 minutes, then remove the satay sauce from the heat and set aside.
4. Season the cod with white pepper.
5. Heat a large nonstick skillet with the remaining 1 tsp olive oil, and add the cod fillets. Cook for 3 minutes, then turn and cook for 3-4 minutes more or until the fish flakes when tested with a fork.
6. Cover the fish with the satay sauce and serve immediately.

Nutritions: Calories: 255; Fat: 10 g (with 35% calories from fat); Saturated fat: 5 g; Monounsaturated fat: 3 g; Carbs: 9 g; Sodium: 222 mg; Dietary fiber: 1 g; Protein: 33 g; Cholesterol: 72 mg
- Vitamin A: 4% DV

Vitamin C: 9% DV; Sugar: 4 g

107. CRISPY MIXED NUT FISH FILLETS

Preparation Time
10 minutes

Cooking Time
15 minutes

Servings
4

INGREDIENTS

- 4 (6 oz) white fish fillets, such as red snapper or cod
- 2 tbsp low-sodium yellow mustard
- 2 tbsp nonfat plain Greek yogurt
- 2 tbsp low-fat buttermilk
- 1 tsp dried Italian herb seasoning
- ⅛ tsp white pepper
- ¼ cup hazelnut flour
- 2 tbsp almond flour
- 2 tbsp ground almonds
- 2 tbsp ground hazelnuts

DIRECTIONS

1. Preheat the oven to 400°F. Line a baking sheet with a fine wire rack and set it aside.
2. Pat the fish dry and place it on a plate.
3. In a shallow bowl, combine the mustard, yogurt, buttermilk, Italian seasoning, and white pepper.
4. On a plate, combine the hazelnut flour and almond flour, add the ground almonds and the ground hazelnuts, and mix well.
5. Coat the fish with the mustard mixture, then coat it with the nut mixture. Place on the prepared baking sheet.
6. Bake the fish for 12–17 minutes, until it flakes when tested with a fork. Serve immediately.

Nutritions: Calories: 256; Fat: 9 g (with 32% calories from fat); Saturated fat: 1 g; Monounsaturated fat: 5 g; Carbs: 4 g; Sodium: 206 mg; Dietary fiber: 2 g; Protein: 38 g; Cholesterol: 63 mg
- Vitamin A: 4% DV

Vitamin C: 6% DV; Sugar: 2 g

108. STEAMED SOLE ROLLS WITH GREENS

Preparation Time: 15 minutes
Cooking Time: 10 minutes
Servings: 4

INGREDIENTS

- 4 (6 oz) sole fillets
- 2 tsp grated peeled fresh ginger root
- 2 garlic cloves, minced
- 2 tsp low-sodium soy sauce
- 1 tbsp rice wine vinegar
- 1 tsp toasted sesame oil
- 2 cup fresh torn spinach leaves
- 1 cup fresh stemmed torn kale
- 1 cup sliced mushrooms
- 2 tsp toasted sesame seeds

DIRECTIONS

1. Cut the sole fillets in half lengthwise. Sprinkle each piece with some ginger root and garlic. Roll up the fillets—ginger root side in. Fasten with a toothpick and set aside.
2. In a small bowl, combine the soy sauce, vinegar, and toasted sesame oil.
3. Bring water to a boil over medium heat in a large shallow saucepan that will hold your steamer.
4. Arrange the spinach leaves and kale at the bottom of the steamer. Add the rolled sole fillets. Add the mushrooms, and sprinkle everything with the soy sauce mixture.
5. Cover and steam for 7–11 minutes or until the fish is cooked and flakes when tested with a fork. Remove the toothpicks.
6. To serve, sprinkle with the sesame seeds and serve the fish on top of the wilted greens and mushrooms.

Nutritions: Calories: 263; Fat: 8 g (with 27% calories from fat); Saturated fat: 2 g; Monounsaturated fat: 3 g; Carbs: 7 g; Sodium: 247 mg; Dietary fiber: 3 g; Protein: 36 g; Cholesterol: 81 mg
- Vitamin A: 81% DV

Vitamin C: 47% DV; Sugar: 0 g

109. RED SNAPPER SCAMPI

Preparation Time: 10 minutes
Cooking Time: 20 minutes
Servings: 4

INGREDIENTS

- 2 tsp olive oil
- 4 garlic cloves, minced
- ¼ cup fresh lemon juice
- ¼ cup white wine or fish stock
- 1 tsp fresh lemon zest
- A pinch of salt
- ⅛ tsp lemon pepper
- 4 (6 oz) red snapper fillets
- 2 scallions, minced
- 3 tbsp minced flat-leaf fresh parsley

DIRECTIONS

1. Preheat the oven to 400°F. Line a baking pan with parchment paper.
2. In a small bowl, combine the olive oil, garlic, lemon juice, white wine, lemon zest, salt, and lemon pepper.
3. Arrange the fillets with the skin-side down (if the skin is attached) on the prepared baking pan. Pour the lemon juice mixture over the fillets.
4. Roast for 15–20 minutes, or until the fish flakes when tested with a fork.
5. Serve the fish with the pan drippings, sprinkled with the scallions and parsley.

Nutritions: Calories: 212; Fat: 5 g (with 21% calories from fat); Saturated fat: 1 g; Monounsaturated fat: 2 g; Carbs: 3 g; Sodium: 112 mg; Dietary fiber: 0 g; Protein: 35 g; Cholesterol: 62 mg
- Vitamin A: 10% DV

Vitamin C: 26% DV; Sugar: 1 g

110. GREEN RICE SALAD WITH TOMATOES

Preparation Time
15 minutes

Cooking Time
10 minutes

Servings
4

INGREDIENTS

- 2 (10 oz) packages of frozen cooked brown rice
- 2 tbsp olive oil
- 2 tbsp fresh lemon juice
- 1 tbsp orange juice
- 1 tbsp pure maple syrup
- A pinch of salt
- ½ cup chopped fresh flat-leaf parsley
- ¼ cup chopped fresh basil leaves
- 1 tbsp fresh thyme leaves
- 1 (10 oz) package of frozen baby peas, thawed
- 1 cup sliced celery
- 2 cup grape tomatoes

DIRECTIONS

1. Thaw the brown rice according to the package directions.
2. Meanwhile, in a large salad bowl, combine the olive oil, lemon juice, orange juice, maple syrup, salt, parsley, basil, and thyme, and mix well.
3. Add the cooked brown rice and toss to coat.
4. Stir in the peas, celery, and tomatoes and toss again. Serve or refrigerate.

Nutritions: Calories: 305; Fat: 9 g (with 27% calories from fat); Saturated fat: 1 g; Monounsaturated fat: 6 g; Carbs: 50 g; Sodium: 133 mg; Dietary fiber: 7 g; Protein: 9 g; Cholesterol: 0 mg
- Vitamin A: 62% DV

Vitamin C: 69% DV; Sugar: 10 g

111. ORANGE THYME RED SNAPPER

Preparation Time 5 minutes

Cooking Time 10 minutes

Servings 4

INGREDIENTS

- 1 medium orange
- 2 tsp olive oil
- 4 (6 oz) fillets of red snapper
- A pinch of salt
- ⅛ tsp white pepper
- 2 tsp olive oil
- 2 scallions, chopped
- 1 ½ tsp fresh thyme leaves, or ½ tsp dried

DIRECTIONS

1. Rinse the orange and dry. Using a small grater or zester, remove 1 tsp zest from the orange and set aside. Cut the orange in half, squeeze in a small bowl, and reserve the juice.
2. Add the olive oil to a large nonstick skillet and place over medium heat. Meanwhile, sprinkle the fish with salt and white pepper.
3. Add the fish to the skillet, skin-side down, if the skin is attached. Cook for 3 minutes on one side, briefly pressing on the fish with a spatula to prevent curling (or slit the fillet to prevent curling). Turn the fish and cook for 2–3 minutes on the second side, until the fish flakes when tested with a fork.
4. Transfer the fish to a plate. Remove the skin, if present, and discard. Cover the fish with a foil tent to keep it warm.
5. Add the scallions and the thyme to the skillet; cook and stir gently for 1 minute. Add the reserved orange juice and orange zest and simmer for 2–3 minutes or until the liquid is slightly reduced.
6. Pour the sauce over the fish and serve immediately.

Nutritions: Calories: 232; Fat: 7 g (with 27% calories from fat); Saturated fat: 1 g; Monounsaturated fat: 4 g; Carbs: 6 g; Sodium: 121 mg; Dietary fiber: 1 g; Protein: 35 g; Cholesterol: 62 mg
- Vitamin A: 7% DV

Vitamin C: 48% DV; Sugar: 5 g

112. FARRO VEGGIE PILAF

Preparation Time: 10 minutes
Cooking Time: 20 minutes
Servings: 4

INGREDIENTS

- 1 cup farro
- 3 cup low-sodium vegetable broth
- 2 tsp olive oil
- 1 onion, chopped
- 3 garlic cloves, minced
- 8 oz sliced cremini mushrooms
- 3 stalks of celery, sliced
- 3 tbsp grated Parmesan cheese
- ⅓ cup chopped fresh flat-leaf parsley
- 1 tbsp minced fresh tarragon

DIRECTIONS

1. In a medium saucepan, combine the farro and vegetable broth, and bring to a boil over medium-high heat. Reduce the heat to low, partially cover the pan, and simmer for 18–22 minutes or until the farro is tender.
2. Meanwhile, in a large nonstick skillet, heat the olive oil. Add the onion and garlic, and cook for 3 minutes, stirring frequently.
3. Add the mushrooms and celery, and cook for 3 minutes, stirring frequently.
4. When the farro is tender, drain it if necessary, and add it to the skillet. Cook and stir for 1 minute.
5. Add the Parmesan cheese, parsley, and tarragon; stir and serve immediately.

Nutritions: Calories: 191; Fat: 5 g (with 24% calories from fat); Saturated fat: 1 g; Monounsaturated fat: 2 g; Carbs: 30 g; Sodium: 188 mg; Dietary fiber: 4 g; Protein: 7 g; Cholesterol: 3 mg
- Vitamin A: 11% DV

Vitamin C: 17% DV; Sugar: 6 g

113. BUCKWHEAT VEGGIE PILAF

Preparation Time: 10 minutes
Cooking Time: 20 minutes
Servings: 4

INGREDIENTS

- 2 tsp olive oil
- 1 cup buckwheat groats (kasha)
- 1 onion, chopped
- 2 garlic cloves, minced
- 1 cup sliced mushrooms
- 1 carrot, peeled and sliced
- 1 cup low-sodium vegetable broth
- 1 cup water
- 1 cup frozen corn
- 1 tomato, chopped
- ½ cup shredded Havarti or Swiss cheese
- ⅓ cup chopped fresh flat-leaf parsley

DIRECTIONS

1. In a large saucepan, heat the olive oil over medium heat. Add the buckwheat, onion, garlic, mushrooms, and carrot, and cook for 3-4 minutes or until the vegetables are crisp-tender.
2. Add the vegetable broth, water, and corn, and bring to a simmer. Reduce heat to low, partially cover, and cook for 12-15 minutes or until the broth is evaporated and the buckwheat is tender.
3. Stir in the tomato, Havarti cheese, and parsley, and serve.

Nutritions: Calories: 333; Fat: 8 g (with 22% calories from fat); Saturated fat: 3 g; Monounsaturated fat: 3 g; Carbs: 58 g; Sodium: 87 mg; Dietary fiber: 7 g; Protein: 13 g; Cholesterol: 12 mg
- Vitamin A: 67% DV

Vitamin C: 44% DV; Sugar: 4 g

114. AMARANTH WITH ARTICHOKES AND GARLIC

Preparation Time
10 minutes

Cooking Time
20 minutes

Servings
4

INGREDIENTS

- 2 ½ cup low-sodium vegetable broth
- 1 cup amaranth
- 2 tsp olive oil
- 1 shallot, minced
- 6 garlic cloves, sliced
- 1 red bell pepper, seeded and chopped
- 1 (15 oz) can of artichoke hearts, drained and chopped
- ½ tsp dried thyme leaves
- ¼ cup grated Parmesan cheese

DIRECTIONS

1. In a large saucepan, bring the vegetable broth to a boil over high heat. Add the amaranth and stir. Cover the pot, reduce the heat to low, and simmer for 15-20 minutes or until the amaranth is tender.
2. Meanwhile, in a large nonstick skillet, heat the olive oil over medium-low heat.
3. Add the shallot and the garlic, and cook and stir for 2 minutes.
4. Add the bell pepper, and cook for 2 minutes. Add the chopped artichoke hearts and thyme and cook for 2 minutes.
5. When the amaranth is tender, drain well and add to the skillet. Add the Parmesan cheese and stir. Serve immediately.

Nutritions: Calories: 301; Fat: 6 g (with 18% calories from fat); Saturated fat: 2 g; Monounsaturated fat: 1 g; Carbs: 48 g; Sodium: 221 mg; Dietary fiber: 11 g; Protein: 15 g; Cholesterol: 5 mg
- Vitamin A: 23% DV

Vitamin C: 49% DV; Sugar: 3 g

115. FRUITED QUINOA SALAD

Preparation Time
10 minutes

Cooking Time
20 minutes

Servings
4

INGREDIENTS

- 1 cup quinoa
- 2 cup water
- 3 tbsp fresh lemon juice
- 1 tbsp pure honey
- 2 tbsp buttermilk
- 2 tbsp chopped fresh mint
- 2 cup red grapes
- 1 cup cherries, pitted
- 2 cup fresh blueberries
- ¼ cup crumbled Goat cheese

DIRECTIONS

1. Put the quinoa in a strainer and rinse well under cool running water.
2. In a medium saucepan, combine the quinoa and the water and bring to a boil over high heat. Reduce the heat to low and simmer for 15-18 minutes or until the liquid is absorbed. Put the quinoa in a salad bowl.
3. Meanwhile, in a small bowl, combine the lemon juice, honey, buttermilk, and mint, and mix well. Pour over the quinoa in the bowl and toss.
4. Add the grapes, cherries, and blueberries and toss to coat. Top with the goat cheese and serve.

Nutritions: Calories: 272; Fat: 4 g (with 13% calories from fat); Saturated fat: 1 g; Monounsaturated fat: 0 g; Carbs: 55 g; Sodium: 43 mg; Dietary fiber: 6 g; Protein: 9 g; Cholesterol: 5 mg
- Vitamin A: 4% DV

Vitamin C: 54% DV; Sugar: 23 g

116. WARM TEFF CHUTNEY SALAD

Preparation Time: 15 minutes
Cooking Time: 15 minutes
Servings: 4

INGREDIENTS

- ¾ cup teff
- ½ cup apple juice
- 1 cup water
- A pinch of salt
- ½ cup mango chutney
- ⅓ cup low-fat plain Greek yogurt
- 2 tbsp fresh lemon juice
- 2 tbsp apple juice
- 2 tsp curry powder
- 1 ½ cup red seedless grapes
- 1 cup sliced celery
- 2 scallions, sliced

DIRECTIONS

1. In a medium saucepan, combine the teff, apple juice, water, and salt over medium-high heat. Bring to a simmer, reduce heat to low, and simmer for 10-15 minutes or until the teff is tender.
2. Meanwhile, to make the dressing, in a large salad bowl combine the chutney, yogurt, lemon juice, apple juice, and curry powder and mix well.
3. Add the teff to the dressing along with the grapes, celery, and scallions. Stir gently to coat, and serve.

Nutritions: Calories: 212; Fat: 1 g (with 4% calories from fat); Saturated fat: 0 g; Monounsaturated fat: 0 g; Carbs: 46 g; Sodium: 91 mg; Dietary fiber: 5 g; Protein: 6 g; Cholesterol: 4 mg
- Vitamin A: 8% DV

Vitamin C: 67% DV; Sugar: 24 g

117. TEFF WITH BROCCOLI PESTO

Preparation Time: 10 minutes
Cooking Time: 20 minutes
Servings: 4

INGREDIENTS

- 3 ½ cup low-sodium vegetable broth, divided
- 1 cup teff
- 1 ½ cup broccoli florets, cut into bite-sized pieces
- 1 cup packed fresh basil leaves
- 2 tbsp olive oil
- 2 tbsp fresh lemon juice
- 2 tbsp grated Romano cheese
- 2 garlic cloves
- A pinch of salt
- ⅛ tsp black pepper

DIRECTIONS

1. In a medium saucepan, bring 2 ½ cups of the vegetable broth to a boil. Add the teff and bring it back to a simmer. Reduce the heat to low and simmer for 15–20 minutes or until the teff is tender.
2. Meanwhile, in another medium saucepan, combine the broccoli and the remaining 1 cup of vegetable broth over medium heat and bring to a simmer. Simmer for 5–7 minutes or until the broccoli is tender. Drain, reserving 2 tbsp vegetable broth.
3. To make the broccoli pesto, put the broccoli in a food processor or blender and add the basil, olive oil, lemon juice, Romano cheese, garlic, reserved vegetable broth, salt, and pepper. Process or blend until the mixture is smooth.
4. Drain the teff, if necessary, and place in a serving bowl.
5. Toss half the broccoli pesto with the teff, and drizzle the remaining broccoli mixture over all. Serve immediately.

Nutritions: Calories: 286; Fat: 9 g (with 28% calories from fat); Saturated fat: 2 g; Monounsaturated fat: 4 g; Carbs: 41 g; Sodium: 168 mg; Dietary fiber: 5 g; Protein: 11 g; Cholesterol: 4 mg
- Vitamin A: 10% DV

Vitamin C: 85% DV; Sugar: 2 g

118. WARM BARLEY SALAD WITH SPRING VEGGIES

Preparation Time 10 minutes

Cooking Time 20 minutes

Servings 4

INGREDIENTS

- 1 cup quick-cooking pearled barley
- 2 ½ cup low-sodium vegetable broth
- 1 tbsp olive oil
- ½ lb asparagus spears, cut into 1-inch pieces, tough stem removed
- 4 scallions, chopped
- 1 cup sugar snap peas
- 2 cup frozen baby peas, thawed
- 2 tbsp fresh lemon juice
- 2 tbsp low-sodium yellow mustard
- 2 tbsp apple juice
- 2 tsp fresh thyme leaves

DIRECTIONS

1. In a large saucepan, combine the barley and broth over medium-high heat and bring to a boil. Reduce the heat to low, partially cover, and simmer until the barley is tender, 10-15 minutes.
2. Meanwhile, heat the olive oil in a large nonstick skillet. Add the asparagus, scallions, and sugar snap peas. Sauté until the vegetables are crisp-tender. Add the baby peas, and cook for 1 minute.
3. In a large serving bowl, combine the lemon juice, mustard, apple juice, and thyme, and mix. Add the sautéed vegetables to the bowl.
4. Drain the barley, if necessary, and add to the bowl along with the sautéed vegetables and dressing. Toss to coat, and serve warm.

Nutritions: Calories: 357; Fat: 5 g (with 13% calories from fat); Saturated fat: 1 g; Monounsaturated fat: 2 g; Carbs: 69 g; Sodium: 103 mg; Dietary fiber: 14 g; Protein: 12 g; Cholesterol: 0 mg
- Vitamin A: 23% DV

Vitamin C: 52% DV; Sugar: 19 g

119. SMASHED BABY POTATOES

Preparation Time
5 minutes

Cooking Time
25 minutes

Servings
4

INGREDIENTS

- 1 lb baby red and yellow potatoes, scrubbed and cut in half
- 1 cup low-sodium vegetable stock
- 2 tbsp low-sodium yellow mustard
- 1 tbsp melted butter
- 1 tbsp lemon juice

DIRECTIONS

1. Preheat the oven to 425°F.
2. Place the potatoes, cut-side down, on a rimmed baking sheet. Pour the stock around the potatoes, and cover the cookie sheet with heavy-duty foil.
3. Roast the potatoes for 18–22 minutes, or until they are tender when pierced with a fork.
4. Meanwhile, in a small bowl, combine the mustard, melted butter, and lemon juice. Mix together and set aside.
5. Take the potatoes out of the oven; turn the oven to broil.
6. Remove the foil and, using a glass or a fork, gently press down on each potato to flatten it. (Don't press so hard you break the potatoes into pieces.)
7. Brush the mustard mixture onto the potatoes.
8. Broil the potatoes 6 inches from the heat source for 2–4 minutes, watching carefully, until they are browned and crisp. Serve immediately.

Nutritions: Calories: 122; Fat: 3 g (with 22% calories from fat); Saturated fat: 2 g; Monounsaturated fat: 1 g; Carbs: 22 g; Sodium: 125 mg; Dietary fiber: 3 g; Protein: 2 g; Cholesterol: 8 mg
- Vitamin A: 2% DV

Vitamin C: 41% DV; Sugar: 2 g

120. SKILLET-ROASTED SWEET POTATOES

Preparation Time
10 minutes

Cooking Time
20 minutes

Servings
4

INGREDIENTS

- 2 medium sweet potatoes
- 1 tbsp fresh lemon juice
- 2 tsp olive oil
- A pinch of salt
- ⅛ tsp white pepper
- 3 tbsp chopped fresh flat-leaf parsley

DIRECTIONS

1. Scrub the sweet potatoes under cool, running water. Cut off any damaged areas. Don't peel the potatoes.
2. Cut the potatoes into bite-sized pieces, and sprinkle with the lemon juice.
3. Heat the olive oil over medium heat in a large nonstick skillet.
4. Add the potatoes, and sprinkle with the salt and white pepper.
5. Cook the potatoes, stirring often, for 15–20 minutes, or until they are tender when pierced with a fork and the outsides are crisp.
6. Remove from the heat, sprinkle with the parsley, and serve immediately.

Nutritions: Calories: 78; Fat: 2 g (with 23% calories from fat); Saturated fat: 0 g; Monounsaturated fat: 2 g; Carbs: 14 g; Sodium: 37 mg; Dietary fiber: 2 g; Protein: 1 g; Cholesterol: 0 mg
- Vitamin A: 189% DV

Vitamin C: 12% DV; Sugar: 3 g

121. MASHED SWEET POTATOES WITH NUT AND SEED TOPPING

Preparation Time
10 minutes

Cooking Time
20 minutes

Servings
4

INGREDIENTS

- 1 (16 oz) bag of diced sweet potatoes
- 1 tsp unsalted butter
- 2 tbsp flaxseed
- 2 tbsp chopped walnuts
- 1 tbsp sesame seeds
- 1 tbsp chia seeds
- ½ tsp ground cinnamon
- ⅛ tsp ground nutmeg
- 3 tbsp natural unsweetened applesauce
- 2 tbsp apple juice
- A pinch of salt

DIRECTIONS

1. Rinse the sweet potatoes. Put them in a large saucepan and add water to cover them. Bring to a boil over high heat; reduce heat to low, partially cover, and simmer for 10-15 minutes or until the potatoes are soft.
2. Meanwhile, heat the butter in a large skillet over medium heat. Add the flaxseed, walnuts, sesame seeds, chia seeds, cinnamon, and nutmeg. Sauté for 2-3 minutes, stirring constantly, until the mixture is fragrant. Transfer the mixture into a small bowl and set aside.
3. When they are soft, drain the potatoes, and put them in a large bowl. Add the applesauce, apple juice, and salt, and mash the potatoes until smooth. Sprinkle with a nut topping and serve.

Nutritions: Calories: 193; Fat: 8 g (with 37% calories from fat); Saturated fat: 1 g; Monounsaturated fat: 1 g; Carbs: 29 g; Sodium: 65 mg; Dietary fiber: 7 g; Protein: 4 g; Cholesterol: 3 mg
- Vitamin A: 318% DV

Vitamin C: 10% DV; Sugar: 7 g

122. GRILLED SWEET POTATOES AND PEPPERS

Preparation Time
16 minutes

Cooking Time
14 minutes

Servings
4

INGREDIENTS

- 2 medium-sized sweet potatoes, peeled
- 1 red bell pepper, seeded and cut into quarters
- 1 yellow bell pepper, seeded and cut into quarters
- 1 orange bell pepper, seeded and cut into quarters
- 1 tbsp pure maple syrup
- 2 tsp olive oil
- A pinch of salt
- ¼ cup chopped fresh basil leaves

DIRECTIONS

1. Prepare and preheat the grill to medium.
2. Slice the sweet potatoes on a diagonal into ¼-inch slices.
3. In a large bowl, combine the sweet potato slices and the bell pepper quarters. Drizzle with maple syrup, olive oil, and salt, and toss.
4. Place the potato slices on the grill, followed by the bell pepper quarters (skin-side down).
5. Cover the grill and cook for 4-5 minutes or until the vegetables have grill marks.
6. Turn the vegetables, cover the grill, and cook for 4-6 minutes until the vegetables have softened. The bell peppers will probably be ready before the sweet potatoes are done, so check them frequently.
7. Remove the veggies from the grill as they cook. Slice the bell peppers into strips before serving.
8. Sprinkle with the basil and serve.

Nutritions: Calories: 117; Fat: 3 g (with 23% calories from fat); Saturated fat: 0 g; Monounsaturated fat: 2 g; Carbs: 22 g; Sodium: 52 mg; Dietary fiber: 4 g; Protein: 2 g; Cholesterol: 0 mg
- Vitamin A: 243% DV

Vitamin C: 193% DV; Sugar: 9 g

123. ONE-POT VEGGIE PASTA

Preparation Time: 15 minutes
Cooking Time: 10 minutes
Servings: 4

INGREDIENTS

- 1 tbsp olive oil
- 1 onion, chopped
- 2 garlic cloves, minced
- 1 (8 oz) package of sliced mushrooms
- 2 yellow bell peppers, seeded and chopped
- 3 tomatoes, cored and chopped
- 1 ¾ cup low-sodium vegetable broth
- 1 tsp dried Italian seasoning
- ⅛ tsp black pepper or cayenne pepper
- 8 oz whole-wheat spaghetti
- 2 cup rinsed arugula
- ¼ cup grated Parmesan cheese

DIRECTIONS

1. Heat a large saucepan over medium heat and add the olive oil.
2. Add the onion, garlic, and mushrooms, and cook and stir for 2–3 minutes.
3. Add the bell peppers and tomatoes, and cook and stir for 3 minutes.
4. Add the broth, Italian seasoning, and black pepper, and bring to a simmer.
5. Add the spaghetti, making sure the pasta is submerged in the cooking liquid. Bring to a simmer and cook for 10–12 minutes, stirring occasionally, until the pasta is cooked al dente.
6. Turn off the heat and stir in the arugula until it is wilted.
7. Serve immediately with the Parmesan cheese sprinkled on top.

Nutritions: Calories: 337; Fat: 7 g (with 19% calories from fat); Saturated fat: 2 g; Monounsaturated fat: 3 g; Carbs: 60 g; Sodium: 228 mg; Dietary fiber: 4 g; Protein: 15 g; Cholesterol: 6 mg
- Vitamin A: 24% DV

Vitamin C: 313% DV; Sugar: 6 g

124. PASTA PUTTANESCA

Preparation Time
15 minutes

Cooking Time
10 minutes

Servings
4

INGREDIENTS

- Water as needed
- 8 oz whole-wheat spaghetti
- 1 tbsp olive oil
- 1 onion, chopped
- 3 garlic cloves, minced
- 2 cup grape tomatoes
- 2 tbsp chopped Kalamata olives
- 1 tbsp capers, rinsed and drained
- 1 tsp anchovy paste
- 1 (14 oz) can of no-salt-added diced tomatoes, undrained
- 3 tbsp no-salt-added tomato paste
- ⅛ tsp red pepper flakes
- 3 tbsp minced fresh basil leaves

DIRECTIONS

1. Bring a large pot of water to a boil. Add the spaghetti and cook until al dente, about 7 minutes. Drain and set aside.
2. Meanwhile, heat the olive oil in a large nonstick skillet over medium heat.
3. Add the onion and garlic, and cook and stir for 3 minutes.
4. Add the grape tomatoes, olives, capers, anchovy paste, diced tomatoes, tomato paste, and red pepper flakes, and bring to a simmer. Simmer for 5 minutes.
5. Add the pasta and toss to combine. Sprinkle with the basil and serve.

Nutritions: Calories: 290; Fat: 5 g (with 16% calories from fat); Saturated fat: 1 g; Monounsaturated fat: 3 g; Carbs: 56 g; Sodium: 167 mg; Dietary fiber: 3 g; Protein: 11 g; Cholesterol: 1 mg
- Vitamin A: 21% DV

Vitamin C: 41% DV; Sugar: 7 g

125. VEGETABLE EGG FRIED RICE

Preparation Time: 15 minutes

Cooking Time: 13 minutes

Servings: 4

INGREDIENTS

- 1 (10 oz) package of frozen cooked brown rice, thawed
- ¼ cup low-sodium vegetable broth
- 2 tsp low-sodium tamari
- 1 tsp hoisin sauce
- 2 eggs
- 2 tsp toasted sesame oil
- 1 onion, chopped
- 3 garlic cloves, minced
- 1 red bell pepper, seeded and chopped
- 2 cup frozen baby peas
- 2 tbsp minced fresh chives

DIRECTIONS

1. Thaw the brown rice according to package directions, and set it aside.
2. In a small bowl, combine the vegetable broth, tamari, and hoisin sauce, and set aside.
3. In a small bowl, beat the eggs.
4. Heat the sesame oil in a large nonstick skillet or wok over medium-high heat. Add the eggs and scramble for 2-3 minutes, stirring frequently. Remove the eggs from the skillet and set them aside.
5. Add the onion, garlic, and bell pepper to the skillet, and stir-fry for 2-3 minutes or until crisp tender.
6. Add the thawed rice and the frozen peas to the skillet, and stir-fry for 4 minutes or until the rice is hot.
7. Add the scrambled eggs and the sauce mixture to the skillet, and stir-fry for 2-3 minutes or until everything is hot. Sprinkle with the chives, and serve immediately.

Nutritions: Calories: 214; Fat: 6 g (with 25% calories from fat); Saturated fat: 1 g; Monounsaturated fat: 2 g; Carbs: 32 g; Sodium: 231 mg; Dietary fiber: 6 g; Protein: 9 g; Cholesterol: 106 mg
- Vitamin A: 50% DV

Vitamin C: 89% DV; Sugar: 7 g

126. TUNA IN POTATOES

Preparation Time
16 minutes

Cooking Time
4 hours

Servings
8

INGREDIENTS

- 4 large potatoes
- 8 oz tuna, canned
- ½ cup cream cheese
- 4 oz Cheddar cheese
- 1 garlic clove
- 1 tsp onion powder
- ½ tsp salt
- 1 tsp ground black pepper
- 1 tsp dried dill

DIRECTIONS

1. Wash the potatoes carefully and cut them into halves.
2. Wrap the potatoes in aluminum foil and place them in the Slow Cooker. Close the Slow Cooker lid and cook the potatoes on high for 2 hours.
3. Meanwhile, peel the garlic clove and mince it. Combine the minced garlic clove with the cream cheese, tuna, salt, ground black pepper, onion powder, and dill.
4. Then shred Cheddar cheese and add it to the mixture.
5. Mix it carefully until homogenous.
6. When the time is over, remove the potatoes from the Slow Cooker and discard the foil only from the flat surface of the potatoes.
7. Then take the fork and mash the flesh of the potato halves gently. Add the tuna mixture to the potato halves and return them to the Slow Cooker.
8. Cook the potatoes for 2 hours more on high. Enjoy!

Nutritions: Calories: 247; Fat: 5.9 g; Fiber: 4 g; Carbs: 3.31 g; Protein: 14 g

127. SHRIMP SCAMPI

Preparation Time: 15 minutes
Cooking Time: 3 hours
Servings: 4

INGREDIENTS

- ¼ cup chicken bone broth
- ½ cup white cooking wine
- 2 tbsp olive oil
- 2 tbsp butter
- 1 tbsp garlic, minced
- 2 tbsp parsley, chopped
- 1 tbsp lemon juice
- Salt and pepper to taste
- 1 lb shrimp, peeled and deveined

DIRECTIONS

1. Mix all the ingredients in your Slow Cooker.
2. Cover the pot.
3. Cook on low for 3 hours.

Nutritions: Calories: 256; Fat: 14.7 g; Sodium: 466 mg; Carbohydrates: 2.1 g; Fiber: 0.1 g; Protein: 23.3 g; Sugar: 2 g

128. SHRIMP BOIL

Preparation Time: 15 minutes
Cooking Time: 4 hours
Servings: 4

INGREDIENTS

- 1 ½ lb potatoes, sliced into wedges
- 2 garlic cloves, peeled
- 2 ears corn
- 1 lb sausage, sliced
- ¼ cup Old Bay seasoning
- 1 tbsp lemon juice
- 2 cup water
- 2 lb shrimp, peeled

DIRECTIONS

1. Put the potatoes in your Slow Cooker. Add the garlic, corn, and sausage in layers.
2. Season with the Old Bay seasoning.
3. Drizzle lemon juice on top.
4. Pour in the water and do not mix.
5. Cover the pot. Cook on high for 4 hours.
6. Add the shrimp on top. Cook for 15 minutes.

Nutritions: Calories: 585; Fat: 25.1 g; Sodium: 2242 mg; Potassium: 1166 mg; Carbohydrates: 3.7 g; Fiber: 4.9 g; Protein: 53.8 g; Sugar: 3.9 g

129. SHRIMP AND SAUSAGE GUMBO

Preparation Time 15 minutes

Cooking Time 1 hour and 15 minutes

Servings 4

INGREDIENTS

- 2 tbsp olive oil
- 2 lb chicken thigh fillet, sliced into cubes
- 2 garlic cloves, crushed and minced
- 1 onion, sliced
- 2 stalks of celery, chopped
- 1 green bell pepper, chopped
- 1 tsp Cajun seasoning
- Salt to taste
- 2 cup beef broth
- 28 oz canned crushed tomatoes
- 4 oz sausage
- 2 tbsp butter
- 1 lb shrimp, peeled and deveined

DIRECTIONS

1. Pour the olive oil into a pan over medium heat.
2. Cook the garlic and chicken for 5 minutes.
3. Add the onion, celery, and bell pepper.
4. Cook until tender.
5. Season with the Cajun seasoning and salt.
6. Cook for 2 minutes.
7. Stir in the sausage, broth, and tomatoes.
8. Cover and cook on low for 1 hour.
9. Add the butter and shrimp to the last 10 minutes of cooking.

Nutritions: Calories: 467; Fat: 33 g; Sodium: 1274 mg; Potassium: 658 mg; Carbohydrates: 5 g; Fiber: 2 g; Protein: 33 g; Sugar: 5 g

130. FISH STEW

Preparation Time
15 minutes

Cooking Time
1 hour and 24 minutes

Servings
2

INGREDIENTS

- 1 lb white fish
- 1 tbsp lime juice
- 2 tbsp olive oil
- 1 onion, sliced
- 2 garlic cloves, sliced
- 1 red pepper, sliced
- 1 jalapeño pepper, sliced
- 1 tsp paprika
- 2 cup chicken broth
- 2 cup tomatoes, chopped
- Salt and pepper to taste
- 2 oz coconut milk

DIRECTIONS

1. Marinate the fish in lime juice for 10 minutes.
2. Pour the olive oil into a pan over medium heat.
3. Add the onion, garlic, and peppers.
4. Cook for 4 minutes.
5. Add the rest of the ingredients except the coconut milk.
6. Cover the pot.
7. Cook on low for 1 hour.
8. Stir in the coconut milk and simmer for 10 minutes.

Nutritions: Calories: 323; Fat: 28.6 g; Sodium: 490 mg; Carbohydrates: 1.1 g; Protein: 9.3 g; Fiber: 3.2 g; Sugar: 6.2 g

131. SALMON WITH LEMON AND DILL

Preparation Time: 15 minutes
Cooking Time: 2 hours
Servings: 4

INGREDIENTS

- Cooking spray
- 1 tsp olive oil
- 2 lb salmon
- 1 tbsp fresh dill, chopped
- Salt and pepper to taste
- 1 garlic clove, minced
- 1 lemon, sliced

DIRECTIONS

1. Spray your Slow Cooker with oil.
2. Brush both sides of the salmon with olive oil.
3. Season the salmon with salt, pepper, dill, and garlic.
4. Add to the Slow Cooker.
5. Put the lemon slices on top.
6. Cover the pot and cook on high for 2 hours.

Nutritions: Calories: 313; Fat: 15.2 g; Sodium: 102 mg; Carbohydrates: 0.7 g; Fiber: 0.1 g; Protein: 44.2 g; Sugar: 0 g

132. DUCK AND BLACKBERRIES

Preparation Time
10 minutes

Cooking Time
25 minutes

Servings
4

INGREDIENTS

- 4 duck breasts, boneless and skin scored
- 2 tbsp balsamic vinegar
- Salt and black pepper to the taste
- 1 cup chicken stock
- 4 oz blackberries
- ¼ cup chicken stock
- 2 tbsp avocado oil

DIRECTIONS

1. Heat a pan with the avocado oil over medium-high heat, add duck breasts skin-side down, and cook for 5 minutes.
2. Flip the duck, add the rest of the ingredients, bring to a simmer, and cook over medium heat for 20 minutes.
3. Divide everything between plates and serve.

Nutritions: Calories: 239; Fat: 10.5 g; Fiber: 10.2 g; Carbs: 21.1 g; Protein: 33.3 g

133. GINGER DUCK MIX

Preparation Time
10 minutes

Cooking Time
1 hour and 50 minutes

Servings
4

INGREDIENTS

- 4 duck legs, boneless
- 4 shallots, chopped
- 2 tbsp olive oil
- 1 tbsp ginger, grated
- 2 tbsp rosemary, chopped
- 1 cup chicken stock
- 1 tbsp chives, chopped

DIRECTIONS

1. In a roasting pan, combine the duck legs with the shallots and the rest of the ingredients except the chives, toss, introduce in the oven at 250°F and bake for 1 hour and 30 minutes.
2. Divide the mix between plates, sprinkle the chives on top, and serve.

Nutritions: Calories: 299; Fat: 10.2 g; Fiber: 9.2 g; Carbs: 18.1 g; Protein: 17.3 g

134. ASPARAGUS SMOKED SALMON

Preparation Time: 15 minutes
Cooking Time: 5 hours
Servings: 6

INGREDIENTS

- 1 tbsp extra-virgin olive oil
- 6 large eggs
- 1 cup heavy (whipping) cream
- 2 tsp chopped fresh dill + additional for garnish
- ½ tsp kosher salt
- ¼ tsp freshly ground black pepper
- 1 ½ cup shredded Havarti or Monterey Jack cheese
- 12 oz asparagus, trimmed and sliced
- 6 oz smoked salmon, flaked

Nutritions: Calories: 388; Fat: 19 g; Carbs: 1.0 g; Protein: 21 g

DIRECTIONS

1. Brush oil into a cooker.
2. Whisk in the heavy cream with eggs, dill, salt, and pepper.
3. Stir in the cheese and asparagus.
4. Gently fold in the salmon and then pour the mixture into the prepared insert.
5. Cover and cook on low or 3 hours on high.
6. Serve warm, garnished with additional fresh dill.

135. SALMON WITH CAPER SAUCE

Preparation Time: 5 minutes
Cooking Time: 45 minutes
Servings: 4

INGREDIENTS

- ½ cup dry white wine
- ½ cup water
- 1 yellow onion, thin sliced
- ½ tsp salt
- ¼ tsp black pepper
- 4 salmon steaks
- 2 tbsp butter
- 2 tbsp flour
- 1 cup chicken broth
- 2 tsp lemon juice
- 3 tbsp capers

DIRECTIONS

1. Combine wine, water, onion, salt, and black pepper in a crockpot; cover and cook on high for 20 minutes.
2. Add salmon steaks; cover and cook on high until salmon is tender or about 20 minutes.
3. To make the sauce, in a small skillet, melt butter over medium flame.
4. Stir in flour and cook for 1 minute. Pour in chicken broth and lemon juice; whisk for 1–2 minutes. Add capers; serve the sauce with salmon.

Nutritions: Calories: 234; Fat: 15 g; Carbs: 2 g; Protein: 12 g

136. VIETNAMESE BRAISED CATFISH

Preparation Time
5 minutes

Cooking Time
6 hours

Servings
3

INGREDIENTS

- 1 fillet of wild-caught catfish, cut into bite-size pieces
- 1 scallion, chopped
- 3 red chilies, chopped
- 1 tbsp grated ginger
- ½ cup swerve sweetener
- 2 tbsp avocado oil
- ¼ cup fish sauce, unsweetened

DIRECTIONS

1. Place a small saucepan over medium heat, add sweetener and cook until it melts.
2. Then add scallion, chilies, ginger, and fish sauce and stir until mixed.
3. Transfer this mixture to a 4-quart Slow Cooker, add fish and toss until coated.
4. Plug in the Slow Cooker, shut it with a lid, and cook for 6 hours at a low heat setting until cooked.
5. Drizzle with avocado oil and serve straight away.

Nutritions: Calories: 156; Fat: 21 g; Protein: 19 g; Carbs: 0.2 g; Fiber: 17 g; Sugar: 0.1 g

137. DUCK, CUCUMBER, AND MANGO SALAD

Preparation Time
10 minutes

Cooking Time
50 minutes

Servings
4

INGREDIENTS

- Zest of 1 orange, grated
- 2 big duck breasts, boneless and skin scored
- 2 tbsp olive oil
- Salt and black pepper to the taste
- 1 tbsp fish sauce
- 1 tbsp lime juice
- 1 garlic clove, minced
- 1 Serrano chili, chopped
- 1 small shallot, sliced
- 1 cucumber, sliced
- 2 mangos, peeled and sliced
- ¼ cup oregano, chopped

DIRECTIONS

1. Heat a pan with the oil over medium-high heat, add the duck breasts skin-side down, and cook for 5 minutes.
2. Add the orange zest, salt, pepper, fish sauce, and the rest of the ingredients, bring to a simmer and cook over medium-low heat for 45 minutes.
3. Divide everything between plates and serve.

Nutritions: Calories: 297; Fat: 9.1 g; Fiber: 10.2 g; Carbs: 20.8 g; Protein: 16.5 g

138. DUCK AND ORANGE WARM SALAD

Preparation Time
10 minutes

Cooking Time
25 minutes

Servings
4

INGREDIENTS

- 2 tbsp balsamic vinegar
- 2 oranges, peeled and cut into segments
- 1 tsp orange zest, grated
- 1 tbsp orange juice
- 3 shallots, minced
- 2 tbsp olive oil
- Salt and black pepper to the taste
- 2 duck breasts, boneless and skin scored
- 2 cup baby arugula
- 2 tbsp chives, chopped

DIRECTIONS

1. Heat a pan with the oil over medium-high heat, add the duck breasts skin-side down, and brown for 5 minutes.
2. Flip the duck, add the shallot, and the other ingredients except for the arugula, orange, and chives, and cook for 15 minutes more.
3. Transfer the duck breasts to a cutting board, cool down, cut into strips, and put in a salad bowl. Add the remaining ingredients, toss, and serve warm.

Nutritions: Calories: 304; Fat: 15.4 g; Fiber: 12.6 g; Carbs: 25.1 g; Protein: 36.4 g

139. CREAMY CORIANDER CHICKEN

Preparation Time
10 minutes

Cooking Time
55 minutes

Servings
4

INGREDIENTS

- 2 chicken breasts, boneless, skinless, and halved
- 2 tbsp avocado oil
- ½ tsp hot paprika
- 1 cup chicken stock
- 1 tbsp almonds, chopped
- 2 spring onions, chopped
- 2 garlic cloves, minced
- ¼ cup heavy cream
- 1 handful coriander, chopped
- Salt and black pepper to the taste

DIRECTIONS

1. Grease a roasting pan with the oil, add the chicken, paprika, and the rest of the ingredients, except the coriander and the heavy cream, toss, introduce in the oven and bake at 360°F for 40 minutes.
2. Add the cream and the coriander, toss, bake for 15 minutes more, divide between plates, and serve.

Nutritions: Calories: 225; Fat: 8.9 g; Fiber: 10.2 g; Carbs: 20.8 g; Protein: 17.5 g

140. LEMONY TURKEY AND PINE NUTS

Preparation Time 10 minutes

Cooking Time 30 minutes

Servings 4

INGREDIENTS

- 2 turkey breasts, boneless, skinless, and halved
- A pinch of salt and black pepper
- 2 tbsp avocado oil
- Juice of 2 lemons
- 1 tbsp rosemary, chopped
- 3 garlic cloves, minced
- ¼ cup pine nuts, chopped
- 1 cup chicken stock

DIRECTIONS

1. Heat a pan with the oil over medium-high heat, add the garlic and the turkey, and brown for 4 minutes on each side.
2. Add the rest of the ingredients, bring to a simmer and cook over medium heat for 20 minutes.
3. Divide the mix between plates and serve with a side salad.

Nutritions: Calories: 293; Fat: 12.4 g; Fiber: 9.3 g; Carbs: 17.8 g; Protein: 24.5 g

141. CREAMY CHICKEN AND MUSHROOMS

Preparation Time
15 minutes

Cooking Time
30 minutes

Servings
4

INGREDIENTS

- 1 red onion, chopped
- 1 tbsp olive oil
- 2 garlic cloves, minced
- 2 carrots chopped
- Salt and black pepper to the taste
- 1 tbsp thyme, chopped
- 1 ½ cup chicken stock
- ½ lb Bella mushrooms, sliced
- 1 cup heavy cream
- 2 chicken breasts, skinless, boneless, and cubed
- 2 tbsp chives, chopped
- 1 tbsp parsley, chopped

DIRECTIONS

1. Heat a Dutch oven with the oil over medium-high heat, add the onion and the garlic and sauté for 5 minutes.
2. Add the chicken and the mushrooms and sauté for 10 minutes more.
3. Add the rest of the ingredients except the chives and the parsley, bring to a simmer, and cook over medium heat for 15 minutes.
4. Add the chives and parsley, divide the mix between plates, and serve.

Nutritions: Calories: 275; Fat: 11.9 g; Fiber: 10.6 g; Carbs: 26.7 g; Protein: 23.7 g

142. OREGANO TURKEY AND PEPPERS

Preparation Time
10 minutes

Cooking Time
1 hour

Servings
4

INGREDIENTS

- 2 red bell peppers, cut into strips
- 2 green bell peppers, cut into strips
- 1 red onion, chopped
- 4 garlic cloves, minced
- ½ cup black olives, pitted and sliced
- 2 cup chicken stock
- 1 big turkey breast, skinless, boneless and cut into strips
- 1 tbsp oregano, chopped
- ½ cup cilantro, chopped

DIRECTIONS

1. In a baking pan, combine the peppers with the turkey and the rest of the ingredients, toss, introduce in the oven at 400°F, and roast for 1 hour.
2. Divide everything between plates and serve.

Nutritions: Calories: 229; Fat: 8.9 g; Fiber: 8.2 g; Carbs: 17.8 g; Protein: 33.6 g

143. TURKEY AND CRANBERRY SAUCE

Preparation Time: 10 minutes
Cooking Time: 50 minutes
Servings: 4

INGREDIENTS

- 1 cup chicken stock
- 2 tbsp avocado oil
- ½ cup cranberry sauce
- 1 big turkey breast, skinless, boneless, and sliced
- 1 yellow onion, roughly chopped
- Salt and black pepper to the taste

DIRECTIONS

1. Heat a pan with the avocado oil over medium-high heat, add the onion and sauté for 5 minutes.
2. Add the turkey and brown for 5 minutes more.
3. Add the rest of the ingredients, toss, introduce in the oven at 350°F, and cook for 40 minutes.

Nutritions: Calories: 382; Fat: 12.6 g; Fiber: 9.6 g; Carbs: 26.6 g; Protein: 17.6 g

144. CHICKEN AND MINT SAUCE

Preparation Time: 10 minutes
Cooking Time: 30 minutes
Servings: 4

INGREDIENTS

- 2 ½ tbsp olive oil
- 2 lb chicken breasts, skinless, boneless, and halved
- 3 tbsp garlic, minced
- 2 tbsp lemon juice
- 1 tbsp red wine vinegar
- ⅓ cup Greek yogurt
- 2 tbsp mint, chopped
- A pinch of salt and black pepper

DIRECTIONS

1. In a blender, combine the garlic with the lemon juice and the other ingredients, except the oil and the chicken, and pulse well.
2. Heat a pan with the oil over medium-high heat, add the chicken, and brown for 3 minutes on each side.
3. Add the mint sauce, introduce it to the oven, and bake everything at 370°F for 25 minutes.
4. Divide the mix between plates and serve.

Nutritions: Calories: 278; Fat: 12 g; Fiber: 11.2 g; Carbs: 18.1 g; Protein: 13.3 g

145. CURRY CHICKEN, ARTICHOKES, AND OLIVES

Preparation Time
5 minutes

Cooking Time
7 hours

Servings
6

INGREDIENTS

- 2 lb chicken breasts, boneless, skinless, and cubed
- 12 oz canned artichoke hearts, drained
- 1 cup chicken stock
- 1 red onion, chopped
- 1 tbsp white wine vinegar
- 1 cup kalamata olives, pitted and chopped
- 1 tbsp curry powder
- 2 tsp basil, dried
- Salt and black pepper to the taste
- ¼ cup rosemary, chopped

DIRECTIONS

1. In your Slow Cooker, combine the chicken with the artichokes, olives, and the rest of the ingredients; put the lid on and cook on low for 7 hours.
2. Divide the mix between plates and serve hot.

Nutritions: Calories: 275; Fat: 11.9 g; Fiber: 7.6 g; Carbs: 19.7 g; Protein: 18.7 g

146. CHILI PRAWNS

Preparation Time
5 minutes

Cooking Time
1 hour

Servings
6

INGREDIENTS

- 18 oz wild-caught prawns, shell-on
- ½ cup sliced scallions
- 1 thumb-sized ginger, minced
- 1 garlic head, peeled and minced
- 1 tbsp swerve sweetener
- 2 tbsp apple cider vinegar
- 2 tbsp Sambal Oelek
- 1 tbsp fish sauce, unsweetened
- 4 tbsp sesame oil
- ½ cup tomato ketchup, keto and unsweetened
- 1 egg, beaten

DIRECTIONS

1. Place all the ingredients, except for prawns, oil, and egg in a 6-quart Slow Cooker and stir until mixed.
2. Plug in the Slow Cooker, shut it with a lid, and cook for 1 hour at a high heat setting.
3. Then add prawns and continue cooking for 15 minutes at a high heat setting or until prawns turn pink.
4. Stir in oil and egg and cook for 10 minutes.
5. Drizzle with more fish sauce and serve.

Nutritions: Calories: 154; Fat: 13 g; Protein: 15 g; Carbs: 3.6 g; Fiber: 17 g; Sugar: 1.7 g

147. TUNA SALPICAO

Preparation Time: 5 minutes

Cooking Time: 3 hours

Servings: 2

INGREDIENTS

- 8 oz cooked wild-caught tuna, cut into inch cubes
- 4 jalapeño peppers, chopped
- 5 red chilies, chopped
- 1 garlic bulb, peeled and minced
- 1 tsp salt
- 1 tsp ground black pepper
- 1 cup avocado oil

DIRECTIONS

1. Place all the ingredients except for tuna in a 4-quart Slow Cooker and stir until mixed.
2. Plug in the Slow Cooker, shut it with a lid, and cook for 4 hours at a low heat setting.
3. Then add tuna and continue cooking for 10 minutes at a high heat setting.
4. Serve straight away.

Nutritions: Calories: 154; Fat: 13 g; Protein: 15 g; Carbs: 1.8 g; Fiber: 17 g; Sugar: 1.0 g

148. SOY-GINGER BRAISED SQUID

Preparation Time
5 minutes

Cooking Time
8 hours

Servings
6

INGREDIENTS

- 18 oz wild-caught squid, cut into rings
- 2 scallions, chopped
- 2 bay leaves
- 1 tbsp grated ginger
- 1 garlic head, peeled and minced
- ½ cup swerve sweetener
- ¼ cup soy sauce
- ¼ cup oyster sauce
- ¼ cup avocado oil
- ¼ cup white wine

DIRECTIONS

1. Plug in a 6-quart Slow Cooker, add all the ingredients, and stir until mixed.
2. Shut with a lid and cook for 8 hours at a low heat setting or until cooked through.
3. Serve straight away.

Nutritions: Calories: 154; Fat: 13 g; Protein: 15 g; Carbs: 3.4 g; Fiber: 17 g; Sugar: 1.9 g

149. SEA BASS IN COCONUT CREAM SAUCE

Preparation Time: 5 minutes
Cooking Time: 1 hour
Servings: 3

INGREDIENTS

- 18 oz wild-caught sea bass
- 5 jalapeño peppers
- 4 stalks of bok choy
- 2 stalks of scallions, sliced
- 1 tbsp grated ginger
- 1½ tsp salt
- 1 tbsp fish sauce, unsweetened
- 2 cup coconut cream

DIRECTIONS

1. Stir together all the ingredients except for bok choy and fish in a bowl and add this mixture to a 6-quarts Slow Cooker.
2. Plug in the Slow Cooker, then add fish, top with bok choy, and shut with a lid.
3. Cook sea bass for 1 hour and 30 minutes or until cooked.
4. Serve straight away.

Nutritions: Calories: 315; Fat: 17 g; Protein: 15 g; Carbs: 2.4 g; Fiber: 17 g; Sugar: 3.2 g

150. COD CHOWDER

Preparation Time: 20 minutes
Cooking Time: 3 hours
Servings: 6

INGREDIENTS

- 1 yellow onion
- 10 oz cod
- 3 oz bacon, sliced
- 1 tsp sage
- 5 oz potatoes
- 1 carrot, grated
- 5 cup water
- 1 tbsp almond milk
- 1 tsp ground coriander
- 1 tsp salt

DIRECTIONS

1. Peel the onion and chop it.
2. Put the chopped onion and grated carrot in the Slow Cooker bowl. Add the sage, almond milk, ground coriander, salt, and water. After this, chop the cod into 6 pieces.
3. Add the fish to the Slow Cooker bowl too. Then chop the sliced bacon and peel the potatoes.
4. Cut the potatoes into cubes.
5. Add the ingredients to the Slow Cooker bowl and close the Slow Cooker lid.
6. Cook the chowder for 3 hours on high. Ladle the prepared cod chowder into the serving bowls.
7. Sprinkle the dish with the chopped parsley if desired. Enjoy!

Nutritions: Calories: 108; Fat: 4.5 g; Fiber: 2 g; Carbs: 3.02 g; Protein: 10 g

DESSERT

151. DESSERT PIZZA

Preparation Time
10 minutes

Cooking Time
30 minutes

Servings
16

INGREDIENTS

- ½ cup unsalted margarine
- ¾ cup brown sugar
- 1 egg yolk
- 1 tsp vanilla
- 1 ½ cup flour
- 1 ¼ cup chocolate chips
- 1 ½ cup miniature marshmallows
- ½ cup dry-roasted peanuts, chopped

DIRECTIONS

1. Preheat the oven to 350°F (180°C, or gas mark 4). Beat the margarine in a large mixing bowl with an electric mixer on medium-high speed for 30 seconds. Add brown sugar and beat until combined. Beat in egg yolk and vanilla until combined.
2. Beat in as much of the flour as you can with the mixer. Stir in any remaining flour with a wooden spoon. Spread dough in a lightly greased 12-inch (30-cm) pizza pan. Bake for 25 minutes, or until golden. Sprinkle hot crust with the chocolate chips.
3. Let stand for 1–2 minutes to soften. Spread chocolate over the crust. Sprinkle with marshmallows and nuts. Bake for 3 minutes more or until marshmallows are puffed and brown. Cool in a pan on a wire rack.

Nutritions: Calories: 247; Protein: 4 g; Carbohydrates: 32 g; Fat: 12 g; Cholesterol: 16 mg; Fiber: 1 g

152. LEMON BISCOTTI

Preparation Time
10 minutes

Cooking Time
40 minutes

Servings
24

INGREDIENTS

- 1 ½ tsp lemon juice
- 2 ½ cup flour
- 1 tsp baking powder
- ¾ cup sugar
- 1 tsp baking soda
- 1 cup egg substitute
- 1 tbsp lemon zest

DIRECTIONS

1. Preheat the oven to 325°F (170°C, or gas mark 3). Sift together flour, baking powder, and baking soda. In another bowl, beat egg substitute and sugar together. (Tip: If you're not into dunking and want a softer cookie, reduce the second baking time to 10 minutes.)
2. Then beat in lemon zest and lemon juice. Add flour mixture to egg mixture and stir until well mixed. On a floured surface, knead the dough for 2 minutes.
3. Divide the dough in half and shape it into 2 logs, about 1 inch (2.5 cm) high and 4 inches (10 cm) wide. Bake for 30 minutes, or until golden brown. Remove from oven and cool. Reduce oven temperature to 300°F (150°C, or gas mark 2).
4. Slice logs diagonally into ½-inch (1.3-cm) thick slices and put the slices back on a baking sheet, cut-side down. Bake for another 20 minutes.

Nutritions: Calories: 81; Protein: 3 g; Carbohydrates: 16 g; Fat: 0 g; Cholesterol: 0 mg; Fiber: 0 g

153. RICE PUDDING WITH DRIED FIGS

Preparation Time
45 minutes

Cooking Time
0 minutes

Servings
2

INGREDIENTS

- 3 cup milk
- 1 cup water
- 2 tbsp sugar
- ⅓ cup white rice, rinsed
- 1 tbsp honey
- 4 dried figs, chopped
- ½ tsp cinnamon
- ½ tsp rose water

DIRECTIONS

1. In a deep saucepan, bring the milk, water, and sugar to a boil until the sugar has dissolved.
2. Stir in the rice, honey, figs, and cinnamon, and turn the heat to a simmer; let it simmer for about 40 minutes, stirring periodically to prevent your pudding from sticking.
3. Afterward, stir in the rose water. Divide the pudding between individual bowls and serve. Bon appétit!

Nutritions: Calories: 228; Fat: 6.1 g; Carbs: 35.1 g; Protein: 7.1 g

154. GREEK PARFAIT WITH MIXED BERRIES

Preparation Time: 10 minutes
Cooking Time: 0 minutes
Servings: 2

INGREDIENTS

- 2 cup Greek yogurt
- 2 cup mixed berries
- ½ cup granola

DIRECTIONS

1. Alternate layers of mixed berries, granola, and yogurt until 2 dessert bowls are filled.
2. Cover and place in your refrigerator until you're ready to serve. Bon appétit!

Nutritions: Calories: 238; Fat: 16.7 g; Carbs: 53 g; Protein: 21.6 g

155. FRUIT KABOBS WITH YOGURT DEEP

Preparation Time: 10 minutes
Cooking Time: 0 minutes
Servings: 2

INGREDIENTS

- 8 clementine orange segments
- 8 medium-sized strawberries
- 8 pineapple cubes
- 8 seedless grapes
- ½ cup Greek-style yogurt
- ½ tsp vanilla extract
- 2 tbsp honey

DIRECTIONS

1. Thread the fruits onto 4 skewers.
2. In a mixing dish, thoroughly combine the yogurt, vanilla, and honey.
3. Serve alongside your fruit kabobs for dipping. Bon appétit!

Nutritions: Calories: 98; Fat: 0.2 g; Carbs: 20.7 g; Protein: 2.8 g

156. NO-BAKE CHOCOLATE SQUARES

Preparation Time: 10 minutes
Cooking Time: 0 minutes
Servings: 2

INGREDIENTS

- 8 oz bittersweet chocolate
- 1 cup tahini paste
- ¼ cup almonds, chopped
- ¼ cup walnuts, chopped

DIRECTIONS

1. Microwave the chocolate for about 30 seconds or until melted. Stir in the tahini, almonds, and walnuts.
2. Spread the batter into a parchment-lined baking pan. Place in your refrigerator until set, for about 3 hours.
3. Cut into squares and serve well-chilled. Bon appétit!

Nutritions: Calories: 198; Fat: 13 g; Carbs: 17.3 g; Protein: 4.6 g

157. STUFFED DRIED FIGS

Preparation Time: 20 minutes
Cooking Time: 0 minutes
Servings: 4

INGREDIENTS

- 12 dried figs
- 2 tbsp honey
- 2 tbsp sesame seeds
- 24 walnut halves

DIRECTIONS

1. Cut off the tough stalk ends of the figs.
2. Slice open each fig.
3. Stuff the fig openings with 2 walnut halves and close.
4. Arrange the figs on a plate, drizzle with honey, and sprinkle sesame seeds on it.
5. Serve.

Nutritions: Calories: 110; Carbs: 26; Fat: 3 g; Protein: 1 g

158. FETA CHEESECAKE

Preparation Time 30 minutes

Cooking Time 90 minutes

Servings 12

INGREDIENTS

- 2 cup Graham Cracker crumbs (about 30 crackers)
- ½ tsp ground cinnamon
- 6 tbsp unsalted butter, melted
- ½ cup sesame seeds, toasted
- 12 oz cream cheese, softened
- 1 cup crumbled Feta cheese
- 3 large eggs
- 1 cup sugar
- 2 cup plain yogurt
- 2 tbsp grated lemon zest
- 1 tsp vanilla

DIRECTIONS

1. Set the oven to 350°F.
2. Mix the cracker crumbs, butter, cinnamon, and sesame seeds with a fork. Move the combination to a springform pan and spread until it is even. Refrigerate.
3. In a separate bowl, mix the cream cheese and Feta. With an electric mixer, beat both kinds of cheese together. Add the eggs one after the other, beating the mixture with each new addition. Add sugar, then keep beating until creamy. Mix in yogurt, vanilla, and lemon zest.
4. Bring out the refrigerated springform and spread the batter on it. Then place it in a baking pan. Pour water into the pan until it is halfway full.
5. Bake for about 50 minutes. Remove cheesecake and allow it to cool. Refrigerate for at least 4 hours.
6. It is done. Serve when ready.

Nutritions: Calories: 98; Carbs: 7 g; Fat: 7 g; Protein: 3 g

159. GREEK-STYLE CHOCOLATE SEMIFREDDO

Preparation Time
15 minutes

Cooking Time
0 minutes

Servings
2

INGREDIENTS

- 3 oz dark chocolate, broken into chunks
- 1 tsp vanilla extract
- A pinch of grated nutmeg
- A pinch of sea salt
- 1 cup heavy cream, divided
- 2 egg whites, at room temperature
- ½ cup caster sugar
- 4 tbsp water
- ½ cup plain Greek yogurt
- 1 tbsp brandy
- 2 tbsp dark chocolate curls, to decorate

DIRECTIONS

1. In a glass bowl, thoroughly combine the chocolate, vanilla, nutmeg, and sea salt.
2. In a small saucepan, bring the cream to a simmer. Pour the hot cream over the chocolate mixture and stir until everything is well incorporated.
3. Place in your refrigerator for about 1 hour.
4. Now, mix the egg whites at high speed until soft peaks form.
5. Dissolve the sugar in water over medium-low heat until a candy thermometer registers 250°F or until the syrup has thickened.
6. Now, pour the syrup into the beaten egg whites and continue to beat until glossy. Fold in the chilled chocolate mixture, Greek yogurt, and brandy; mix again until everything is well combined.
7. Freeze your dessert for at least 3 hours. Then, let it sit at room temperature for about 15 minutes before slicing and serving. Top with the chocolate curls. Bon appétit!

Nutritions: Calories: 517; Fat: 27.7 g; Carbs: 61 g; Protein: 6.8 g

160. TRADITIONAL ITALIAN CAKE WITH ALMONDS

Preparation Time
45 minutes

Cooking Time
0 minutes

Servings
2

INGREDIENTS

- 4 ripe peaches, peeled, pitted, and sliced
- 1 tbsp fresh lemon juice
- 2 ¼ cup all-purpose flour
- 1 tsp baking soda
- ½ tsp baking powder
- A pinch of grated nutmeg
- A pinch of sea salt
- ½ tsp ground cloves
- ½ tsp ground cinnamon
- ½ cup olive oil
- 1 ⅓ cup sugar
- 3 eggs, at room temperature
- 1 cup Greek yogurt
- 1 tsp pure vanilla extract
- ½ cup almonds, chopped

DIRECTIONS

1. Begin by preheating your oven to 350°F. Toss the peaches with lemon juice and set them aside.
2. Then, thoroughly combine the dry ingredients.
3. Then, beat the olive oil and sugar using your mixer at low speed.
4. Gradually fold in the eggs, one at a time, and continue to mix for a few minutes more until it has thickened. Add in the yogurt and vanilla, and mix again.
5. Add the wet mixture to the dry ingredients and stir until you get a thick batter. Fold in the almonds and stir to combine well.
6. Spoon the batter into a parchment-lined baking pan and level the top using a wooden spoon.
7. Bake in the preheated oven for about 40 minutes or until a tester comes out dry and clean. Let it cool on a wire rack before slicing and serving. Bon appétit!

Nutritions: Calories: 407; Fat: 14.7 g; Carbs: 61.4 g; Protein: 6.6 g

161. PEAR CROUSTADE

Preparation Time: 30 minutes
Cooking Time: 60 minutes
Servings: 10

INGREDIENTS

- 1 cup + 1 tbsp all-purpose flour, divided
- 4 ½ tbsp sugar, divided
- ⅛ tsp salt
- 6 tbsp unsalted butter, chilled, cut into ½-inch cubes
- 1 large-sized egg, separated
- 1 ½ tbsp ice-cold water
- 3 firm, ripe pears (Bosc), peeled, cored, sliced into ¼-inch slices
- 1 tbsp fresh lemon juice
- ⅓ tsp ground allspice
- 1 tsp anise seeds

DIRECTIONS

1. Pour 1 cup flour, 1 ½ tbsp sugar, butter, and salt into a food processor and combine the ingredients by pulsing.
2. Whisk the yolk of the egg and ice water in a separate bowl. Mix the egg mixture with the flour mixture. It will form a dough, wrap it, and set aside for an hour.
3. Set the oven to 400°F.
4. Mix the pear, sugar, leftover flour, allspice, anise seed, and lemon juice in a large bowl to make a filling.
5. Arrange the filling in the center of the dough.
6. Bake for about 40 minutes. Cool for about 15 minutes before serving.

Nutritions: Calories: 498; Carbs: 32 g; Fat: 32 g; Protein: 18 g

162. KOURABIEDES ALMOND COOKIES

Preparation Time
20 minutes

Cooking Time
50 minutes

Servings
20

INGREDIENTS

- 1 ½ cup unsalted butter, clarified, at room temperature
- 2 cup confectioner's sugar, divided
- 1 large egg yolk
- 2 tbsp brandy
- 1 ½ tsp baking powder
- 1 tsp vanilla extract
- 5 cup all-purpose flour, sifted
- 1 cup roasted almonds, chopped

DIRECTIONS

1. Preheat the oven to 350°F.
2. Thoroughly mix butter and ½ cup sugar in a bowl. Add in the egg after a while. Create a brandy mixture by mixing the brandy and baking powder. Add the mixture to the egg, add vanilla, then keep beating until the ingredients are properly blended.
3. Add flour and almonds to make a dough.
4. Roll the dough to form crescent shapes. You should be able to get about 40 pieces. Place the pieces on a baking sheet, then bake in the oven for 25 minutes.
5. Allow the cookies to cool, then coat them with the remaining confectioner's sugar.
6. Serve.

Nutritions: Calories: 102; Carbs: 10 g; Fat: 7 g; Protein: 2 g

163. REVANI SYRUP CAKE

Preparation Time
30 minutes

Cooking Time
3 hours

Servings
24

INGREDIENTS

- 1 tbsp unsalted butter
- 2 tbsp all-purpose flour
- 1 cup ground rusk or breadcrumbs
- 1 cup fine semolina flour
- ¾ cup ground toasted almonds
- 3 tsp baking powder
- 16 large eggs
- 2 tbsp vanilla extract
- 3 cup sugar, divided
- 3 cup water
- 2-inch strips of lemon peel, pith removed
- 3 tbsp fresh lemon juice

DIRECTIONS

1. Preheat the oven to 350°F. Grease the baking pan with 1 tbsp butter and flour.
2. Mix the rusk, almonds, semolina, and baking powder in a bowl.
3. In another bowl, mix the eggs, 1 cup sugar, and vanilla, and whisk with an electric mixer for about 5 minutes. Add the semolina mixture to the eggs and stir.
4. Pour the stirred batter into the greased baking pan and place it in the preheated oven.
5. With the remaining sugar, lemon peels, and water make the syrup by boiling the mixture on medium heat. Add the lemon juice after 6 minutes, then cook for 3 minutes. Remove the lemon peels and set the syrup aside.
6. After the cake is done in the oven, spread the syrup over the cake.
7. Cut the cake as you please and serve.

Nutritions: Calories: 348; Carbs: 55 g; Fat: 9 g; Protein: 5 g

164. ALMONDS AND OATS PUDDING

Preparation Time
10 minutes

Cooking Time
15 minutes

Servings
4

INGREDIENTS

- 1 tbsp lemon juice
- Zest of 1 lime
- 1 ½ cup almond milk
- 1 tsp almond extract
- ½ cup oats
- 2 tbsp stevia
- ½ cup silver almonds, chopped

DIRECTIONS

1. In a pan, blend the almond milk, the lime zest, and the other ingredients, whisk, bring to a simmer, and cook over medium heat for 15 minutes.
2. Split the mix into bowls then serve cold.

Nutritions: Calories: 174; Fat: 12.1 g; Fiber: 3.2 g; Carbs: 3.9 g; Protein: 4.8 g

165. MEDITERRANEAN TOMATO SALAD WITH FETA AND FRESH HERBS

Preparation Time
10 minutes

Cooking Time
15 minutes

Servings
2

INGREDIENTS

- 5 diced tomatoes
- 2 oz crumbled Feta cheese
- ½ cup chopped fresh dill
- ½ cup diced onion
- 6 chopped mint leaves
- ½ tsp paprika
- 3 tbsp olive oil
- 2 tbsp minced garlic
- 2 tsp lemon juice
- 2 tsp white wine vinegar
- Salt and black pepper to taste

DIRECTIONS

1. Combine the onions, tomatoes, herbs, and garlic in a bowl, then season with your spices (salt, black pepper, paprika).
2. To create the dressing, in a separate bowl first mix together the olive oil, vinegar, and lemon juice.
3. Top with Feta cheese.

Nutritions: Calories: 125; Protein: 2 g; Carbohydrates: 8 g; Fat: 9 g

166. QUINOA BOWL WITH YOGURT, DATES, AND ALMONDS

Preparation Time
10 minutes

Cooking Time
15 minutes

Servings
2

INGREDIENTS

- 1 ½ cup water
- 1 cup quinoa
- 2 cinnamon sticks
- 1-inch knob of ginger, peeled
- ¼ tsp kosher salt
- 1 cup plain Greek yogurt
- ½ cup dates, pitted and chopped
- ½ cup almonds (raw or roasted), chopped
- 2 tsp honey (optional)

DIRECTIONS

1. Bring the water, quinoa, cinnamon sticks, ginger, and salt to a boil in a medium saucepan over high heat.
2. Reduce the heat to a simmer and cover; simmer for 10-12 minutes. Remove the cinnamon sticks and ginger. Fluff with a fork.
3. Add the yogurt, dates, and almonds to the quinoa and mix them together. Divide evenly among 4 bowls and garnish with ½ tsp honey per bowl, if desired.

Substitution tip: Use any nuts or seeds you like in place of the almonds.

Nutritions: Calories: 125; Protein: 2 g; Carbohydrates: 8 g; Fat: 9 g

167. ALMOND BUTTER BANANA CHOCOLATE SMOOTHIE

Preparation Time
5 minutes

Cooking Time
30 minutes

Servings
2

INGREDIENTS

- ¾ cup almond milk
- ½ medium banana, preferably frozen
- ¼ cup frozen blueberries
- 1 tbsp almond butter
- 1 tbsp unsweetened cocoa powder
- 1 tbsp chia seeds

DIRECTIONS

1. In a blender or Vitamix, add all the ingredients.
2. Blend to combine.

Substitution tip: Peanut butter, sunflower seed butter, and other nut butter are good choices to replace almond butter.

Nutritions: Calories: 125; Protein: 2 g; Carbohydrates: 8 g; Fat: 9 g

168. LOUKOUMADES (FRIED HONEY BALLS)

Preparation Time: 20 minutes
Cooking Time: 45 minutes
Servings: 10

INGREDIENTS

- 2 cup sugar
- 1 cup water
- 1 cup honey
- 1 ½ cup tepid water
- 1 tbsp brown sugar
- ¼ cup vegetable oil
- 1 tbsp active dry yeast
- 1 ½ cup all-purpose flour
- 1 cup cornstarch
- ½ tsp salt
- Vegetable oil for frying
- 1 ½ cup chopped walnuts
- ¼ cup ground cinnamon

DIRECTIONS

1. Boil the sugar and water on medium heat. Add honey after 10 minutes. Cool and set aside.
2. Mix the tepid water, oil, brown sugar, and yeast in a large bowl. Allow it to sit for 10 minutes. In a distinct bowl, blend the flour, salt, and cornstarch. With your hands mix the yeast and the flour to make a wet dough. Cover and set aside for 2 hours.
3. Fry in oil at 350°F. Use your palm to measure the size of each dough as they are dropped into the frying pan. Fry each batch for about 3-4 minutes.
4. Immediately after the loukoumades are done frying, drop them in the prepared syrup.
5. Serve with cinnamon and walnuts.

Nutritions: Calories: 355; Carbs: 64 g; Fat: 7 g; Protein: 6 g

169. CRÈME CARAMEL

Preparation Time: 60 minutes

Cooking Time: 60 minutes

Servings: 12

INGREDIENTS

- 5 cup whole milk
- 2 tsp vanilla extract
- 8 large egg yolks
- 4 large-sized eggs
- 2 cup sugar, divided
- ¼ cup water

DIRECTIONS

1. Preheat the oven to 350°F.
2. Heat the milk with medium heat and wait for it to be scalded.
3. Mix 1 cup sugar, vanilla, and egg yolks in a bowl and add it to the eggs.
4. With a nonstick pan on high heat, boil the water and remaining sugar. Do not stir, instead whirl the pan. When the sugar forms caramel, divide it into ramekins.
5. Divide the egg mixture into the ramekins and place in a baking pan. Increase water to the pan until it is half full. Bake for 30 minutes.
6. Remove the ramekins from the baking pan, cool, then refrigerate for at least 8 hours.
7. Serve.

Nutritions: Calories: 110; Carbs: 21 g; Fat: 1 g; Protein: 2 g

170. FRUITCAKE

Preparation Time: 10 minutes
Cooking Time: 60 minutes
Servings: 12

INGREDIENTS

- ½ cup unsweetened applesauce
- 2 cup assorted dried chopped fruit, such as dates, currants, cherries, or figs
- ½ cup pineapple stored in juice; crushed, drained
- 2 tbsp real vanilla extract
- Zest and juice of 1 medium orange
- ½ cup unsweetened apple juice
- ½ cup chopped or crushed walnuts
- Zest and juice of 1 lemon
- ½ cup rolled oats
- ¼ cup sugar
- 1 cup pastry flour, whole-wheat
- ¼ cup flaxseed flour
- ½ tsp baking powder
- 1 egg
- ½ tsp baking soda

DIRECTIONS

1. Combine the applesauce, dried fruit, fruit zests, pineapple, juices, and vanilla in a medium mixing bowl. Allow 15-20 minutes to soak. Using parchment (baking) paper, line the base of a 9x4-inch pan.
2. Whisk baking soda, oats, sugar, flour, and baking powder in a large mixing bowl. Stir together the fruit and liquid combined with the dry ingredients. Add walnuts and egg to a mixing bowl.
3. Fill the loaf pan halfway with batter and bake for 1 hour, or until the toothpick inserted in the middle comes out clean. Allow the fruitcake to cool in the pan for 30 minutes before removing it.

Nutritions: Calories: 229; Protein: 5 g; Carbohydrates: 41 g; Fat: 5 g; Cholesterol: 41 mg; Fiber: 1 g

171. FRUITED RICE PUDDING

Preparation Time
10 minutes

Cooking Time
50 minutes

Servings
8

INGREDIENTS

- 1 cup brown rice, long-grain
- 2 cup water
- ½ cup brown sugar
- 4 cup fat-free milk
- 1 tsp vanilla extract
- ½ tsp lemon zest
- ¼ cup crushed pineapple
- 6 egg whites
- ¼ cup chopped dried apricots
- ¼ cup raisins

DIRECTIONS

1. Boil 2 cup of water in a saucepan. Cook for 10 minutes after adding the rice. Fill a colander halfway with water and drain completely.
2. Add brown sugar and evaporated milk to the same pot. Cook until heated. Add lemon zest, cooked rice, and vanilla. Simmer for 30 minutes over low heat or until the stew is thick and the rice is soft. Remove from the heat and set aside to cool.
3. Whisk the egg whites together in a small dish. Pour it over the rice mixture. Add raisins, pineapple, and apricots. Stir until everything is thoroughly combined.
4. Preheat the oven to 325°F. Fill the baking dish halfway with the pudding and fruit mixture. Using cooking spray, lightly coat the baking dish. Bake for 20 minutes or until the pudding is set. Warm or chilly is OK.

Nutritions: Calories: 257; Protein: 17 g; Carbohydrates: 48 g; Fat: 1 g; Cholesterol: 5 mg; Fiber: 2.7 g

172. SAUTEED BANANAS

Preparation Time
30 minutes

Cooking Time
30 minutes

Servings
6

INGREDIENTS

For the sauce:
- 1 tbsp honey
- 1 tbsp walnut oil
- 2 tbsp brown sugar, firmly packed
- 1 tbsp golden raisins or dark raisins (sultanas)
- 1 tbsp butter
- 3 tbsp 1% milk, low-fat

For the sauté:
- 2 tbsp dark rum
- ½ tsp canola oil
- 4 firm bananas, about 1 lb

DIRECTIONS

1. Begin by preparing the sauce. Melt the butter in a small saucepan over medium heat. Add honey, walnut oil, and brown sugar. Cook, constantly stirring, for 3 minutes, or until the sugar has dissolved. Cook, constantly stirring, until the sauce thickens slightly, for approximately 3 minutes after adding 1 tbsp milk at a time. Remove the pan from heat and add the raisins. Remove from the oven and keep warm.
2. Peel the bananas and cut each one into 3 pieces crosswise. Each piece should be cut in half lengthwise. Place a nonstick large frying pan over medium-high heat and lightly cover with canola oil. Add bananas and cook for 3-4 minutes or brown. Keep warm by transferring to a platter.
3. Add rum to the pan, get it to a boil, and deglaze the pan, scraping up any browned pieces from the bottom with a wooden spoon. Cook for 30-45 seconds, or until the liquid has been reduced by half. To reheat the bananas, return them to the pan.
4. Divide the bananas into separate dishes or plates to serve. Serve immediately with the heated sauce drizzled over the top.

Nutritions: Calories: 145; Protein: 1 g; Carbohydrates: 27 g; Fat: 5 g; Cholesterol: 5 mg; Fiber: 2.4 g

173. BANANA MOUSSE

Preparation Time: 5 minutes
Cooking Time: 0 minutes
Servings: 4

INGREDIENTS

- 1 tsp vanilla
- 4 tsp sugar
- 1 medium banana; cut into quarters
- 8 slices of banana (¼-inch)
- 2 tbsp low-fat milk
- 1 cup low-fat plain yogurt

DIRECTIONS

1. Combine the vanilla, sugar, milk, and banana in a blender. Blend at high speed for 15 seconds or until smooth. Pour the mixture into a small mixing dish and stir in the yogurt.
2. Chill. Before serving, spoon into 4 dessert plates and top with 2 banana slices for each.

Nutritions: Calories: 94; Protein: 1 g; Carbohydrates: 18 g; Fat: 1 g; Cholesterol: 4 mg; Fiber: 1.4 g

174. WACKY CHOCOLATE CAKE

Preparation Time
5 minutes

Cooking Time
35 minutes

Servings
18

INGREDIENTS

- 3 tbsp cocoa powder; unsweetened
- 1 cup sugar
- 2 ¼ tsp baking soda
- 3 cup pastry flour; whole-wheat
- ½ tsp salt
- 2 tbsp vinegar
- 1 tbsp vanilla
- 2 cup water
- ½ cup canola oil

DIRECTIONS

1. Preheat the oven to 350°F. In a 9x13-inch ungreased baking pan, combine sugar, flour, salt, cocoa powder, and baking soda. Toss them together with a whisk.
2. Make 3 holes in the dry mixture using a spoon. Pour the vanilla extract into one of the holes. Fill another hole with vinegar. Fill the third hole with oil.
3. Microwave the water for 3 minutes on high, or until it boils. Pour boiling water over the contents in the pan gently and evenly. Mix them for about 2 minutes with the whisk. There should be no traces of dry ingredients left.
4. Bake for 25-30 minutes, or until the tester inserted in the middle comes out clean. Allow the cake to finish cooking. Serve after cutting into 18 squares.

Nutritions: Calories: 183; Protein: 3 g; Carbohydrates: 27 g; Fat: 7 g; Cholesterol: 0 mg; Fiber: 1 g

175. VANILLA POACHED PEACHES

Preparation Time
5 minutes

Cooking Time
15 minutes

Servings
4

INGREDIENTS

- ½ cup sugar
- 1 cup water
- 1 split and scraped vanilla bean
- Mint leaves/cinnamon, for garnish
- 4 large pitted and quartered peaches

DIRECTIONS

1. Combine the vanilla bean, sugar, and water in a saucepan.
2. Stir the mixture over low heat until the sugar melts.
3. Continue to cook, occasionally stirring, until the mixture thickens; it will take approximately 10 minutes.
4. Fill tiny ornamental dishes halfway with peaches and sauce. Toss in the chopped fruit.
5. Cook for approximately 5 minutes over low heat.
6. Mint leaves and a sprinkling of cinnamon may be used as a garnish. Serve right away.

Nutritions: Calories: 156; Protein: 1 g; Carbohydrates: 38 g; Fat: Traces,; Cholesterol: 0 mg; Fiber: 2 g

176. BERRY COBBLER

Preparation Time
10 minutes

Cooking Time
35 minutes

Servings
8

INGREDIENTS

- 2 tbsp cornstarch
- ½ cup water, divided
- 1 ½ cup sugar, divided
- 1 tbsp lemon juice
- 1 tsp baking powder
- 4 cup blackberries
- 1 cup flour
- 3 tbsp unsalted margarine

DIRECTIONS

1. Preheat the oven to 400°F (200°C, or gas mark 6). In a saucepan, stir together the cornstarch and ¼ cup (60 ml) cold water until cornstarch is completely dissolved. Add 1 cup (200 g) sugar, lemon juice, and blackberries; combine gently.
2. Combine the flour, remaining sugar, and baking powder in a bowl. Blend in the margarine until the mixture resembles a coarse meal. Boil the remaining ¼ cup (60 ml) water and stir into the flour mixture until it just forms a dough.
3. Transfer the blackberry mixture to a 1 ½-quart (1.4-L) baking dish. Drop spoonful of the dough carefully onto the berries and bake the cobbler on a baking sheet in the middle of the oven for 20-25 minutes, or until the topping is golden.

Nutritions: Calories: 280; Protein: 3 g; Carbohydrates: 59 g; Fat: 5 g; Cholesterol: 0 mg; Fiber: 4 g

177. CARROT AND SPICE QUICK BREAD

Preparation Time
15 minutes

Cooking Time
45 minutes

Servings
17

INGREDIENTS

- 1 cup whole-wheat flour
- 1 tsp grated orange rind
- ½ cup sifted all-purpose flour
- 1 tbsp walnuts, finely chopped
- ¼ cup and 2 tbsp brown sugar, firmly packed
- ½ tsp ground cinnamon
- 1 ½ cup shredded carrots
- ¼ tsp ground ginger
- ½ tbsp golden raisins
- ½ tsp baking soda
- ⅓ cup skim milk
- 1 beaten egg white/egg substitute equal to 1 egg
- 1 tsp vanilla extract
- ¾ tbsp unsweetened orange juice
- ⅓ cup softened trans-fat-free margarine
- ½ tsp baking powder

DIRECTIONS

1. Preheat the oven to 375°F. Coat a 2.5x4.5x8.5-inch loaf pan with cooking spray.
2. Combine the dry ingredients (flour, baking soda, powder, cinnamon, and ginger) in a small dish and set them aside.
3. In a large mixing bowl, blend margarine and sugar using an electric mixer or by hand. Add orange juice, milk, vanilla, egg, and orange rind to a mixing bowl. Stir in raisins, carrots, and walnuts in a mixing bowl. Add dry ingredients that have been set aside. Mix thoroughly.
4. Preheat the oven to 350°F and bake for about 45 minutes, or until a wooden pick inserted in the middle comes out clean. Pour the batter into the loaf pan. Allow 10 minutes to cool in the pan. Remove the pan from the oven and cool fully on a wire rack.

Nutritions: Calories: 110; Protein: 2 g; Carbohydrates: 15 g; Fat: 5 g; Cholesterol: Traces; Fiber: 1 g

178. GRAPES AND LEMON SOUR CREAM SAUCE

Preparation Time
10 minutes

Cooking Time
0 minutes

Servings
6

INGREDIENTS

- 2 tbsp powdered sugar
- ½ cup fat-free sour cream
- ½ tsp lemon zest
- ⅛ tsp vanilla extract
- ½ tsp lemon juice
- 1 ½ cup seedless red grapes
- 3 tbsp chopped walnuts
- 1 ½ cup seedless green grapes

DIRECTIONS

1. Combine lemon juice, powdered sugar, sour cream, lemon zest, and vanilla in a small mixing bowl. To ensure an equal distribution of ingredients, whisk them together. Refrigerate for several hours after covering.
2. In 6 stemmed dessert cups or bowls, place equal parts of grapes and top each dish with a dollop of sauce and ½ spoonful of chopped walnuts. Serve right away.

Nutritions: Calories: 106; Protein: 2 g; Carbohydrates: 208 g; Fat: 2 g; Cholesterol: 2 mg; Fiber: 1 g

179. ORANGE DREAM SMOOTHIE

Preparation Time
10 minutes

Cooking Time
0 minutes

Servings
4

INGREDIENTS

- 1 ½ cup chilled orange juice
- 1 tsp grated orange zest
- 1 cup soy milk, light vanilla, chilled
- ⅓ cup soft or silken tofu
- 1 tbsp dark honey
- ½ tsp vanilla extract
- 4 peeled orange segments
- 5 ice cubes

DIRECTIONS

1. Combine in the blender soy milk, orange juice, vanilla, tofu, orange zest, honey, and ice cubes. Blend for approximately 30 seconds or until smooth and foamy.
2. Pour into long chilled glasses, and garnish each glass with an orange segment.

Nutritions: Calories: 101; Protein: 3 g; Carbohydrates: 20 g; Fat: 1 g; Cholesterol: 0 mg; Fiber: 1 g

180. RUSTIC APPLE-CRANBERRY TART

Preparation Time
10 minutes

Cooking Time
50 minutes

Servings
8

INGREDIENTS

For the filling:
- ¼ cup apple juice
- ½ cup dried cranberries
- ¼ tsp ground cinnamon
- 2 tbsp cornstarch
- 1 tsp vanilla extract
- 4 large cored, peeled, sliced tart apples

For the crust:
- 2 tsp sugar
- 1 ¼ cup whole-wheat flour (whole-meal)
- ¼ cup ice water
- 3 tbsp trans-free margarine

DIRECTIONS

1. Combine the apple juice and cranberries in a small microwave-safe bowl. Cook for 1 minute on high, then stir. Cover and leave aside for 1 hour, or until mixture is near to room temperature. Continue to cook the apple juice for 30 seconds at a time, tossing after each interval, until it is extremely warm.
2. Preheat the oven to 375°F. Combine the apple slices and cornstarch in a large mixing bowl. Toss well to get an equal coating. Add juice and cranberries to a mixing bowl. Mix thoroughly. Add cinnamon and vanilla to a mixing bowl. Put it aside.
3. In a large mixing bowl, combine flour and sugar to make the crust. Add sliced margarine into the mixture and mix well until crumbly. Add 1 tbsp ice water and stir with a fork until the dough forms a rough lump.
4. Place a big sheet of aluminum foil on the surface and tape it down. It should be dusted with flour. Flatten the dough in the middle of the foil. Roll the dough from the center to the edges with a rolling pin to form a 13-inch-diameter circle. Add fruit filling in the dough's middle. Cover the dough with the filling, leaving about a 1-2-inch border. Fold the crust's top and bottom edges up over the filling. The pastry will not completely cover the contents; it should have a rustic appearance.
5. Remove the foil and the countertop from the tape. Cover the tart with another piece of foil to cover the exposed fruit. Slide the tart onto a baking sheet, top and bottom foil included, and bake for 30 minutes. Remove the foil from the top and bake for another 10 minutes or until browned. Serve immediately after cutting into 8 wedges.

Nutritions: Calories: 197; Protein: 3 g; Carbohydrates: 35 g; Fat: 5 g; Cholesterol: 0 mg; Fiber: 5 g

181. STRAWBERRIES AND CREAM

Preparation Time
10 minutes

Cooking Time
0 minutes

Servings
6

INGREDIENTS

- ½ cup brown sugar
- 1 ½ cup fat-free sour cream
- 1 quart fresh hulled and halved strawberries
- 6 whole strawberries for garnish
- 2 tbsp amaretto liqueur

DIRECTIONS

1. Whisk the brown sugar, sour cream, and liqueur in a small bowl.
2. Combine the sour cream mixture and halved strawberries in a large mixing bowl. To combine, carefully stir everything together. Cover and chill for 1 hour or until well cooked.
3. Fill 6 chilled sherbet glasses or colored bowls halfway with strawberries. Serve immediately with whole strawberries as a garnish.

Nutritions: Calories: 136; Protein: 3 g; Carbohydrates: 31 g; Fat: Traces; Cholesterol: 6 mg; Fiber: 5 g

182. WHOLE-GRAIN BANANA BREAD

Preparation Time: 20 minutes
Cooking Time: 60 minutes
Servings: 14

INGREDIENTS

- ½ cup amaranth flour
- ½ cup brown rice flour
- ½ cup millet flour
- ½ cup tapioca flour
- 1 tsp baking soda
- ½ cup quinoa flour
- ⅛ tsp salt
- ½ tsp baking powder
- 2 tbsp grapeseed oil
- ¾ cup egg substitute (egg whites)
- 2 cup mashed banana
- ½ cup raw sugar
- Cooking spray

DIRECTIONS

1. Preheat the oven to 350°F. Spray a 5x9-inch loaf pan lightly with cooking spray before using. Sprinkle with a pinch of flour. Put it aside.
2. Combine all dry ingredients (excluding sugar) in a large mixing bowl. Combine oil, sugar, egg, and mashed banana in a separate bowl. Mix thoroughly. Combine the wet and dry ingredients in a large mixing bowl. Fill the loaf pan halfway with batter and bake for 50-60 minutes.
3. Check the doneness with a toothpick—there should be no batter stuck to it when you remove it. Remove the bread from the oven when done, let it cool, then slice and serve.

Nutritions: Calories: 163; Protein: 4 g; Carbohydrates: 30 g; Fat: 3 g; Cholesterol: 0 mg g,; Fiber: 4.5 g

183. HONEY GRILLED APPLES

Preparation Time
10 minutes

Cooking Time
20 minutes

Servings
4

INGREDIENTS

- 4 apples
- 1 tbsp honey
- 2 tbsp lemon juice
- 1 tbsp unsalted margarine

DIRECTIONS

1. Core apples and cut slices through the skin to make each apple resemble orange sections. Mix the honey, lemon juice, and margarine.
2. Spoon mixture into apple cores. Wrap apples in greased heavy-duty aluminum foil, fold up, and seal. Grill until tender, about 20 minutes.

Nutritions: Calories: 104; Protein: 0 g; Carbohydrates: 21 g; Fat: 3 g; Cholesterol: 0 mg; Fiber: 2 g

184. APPLE TAPIOCA

Preparation Time
5 minutes

Cooking Time
3-4 hours

Servings
4

INGREDIENTS

- 4 cup apples, peeled and sliced
- ½ cup brown sugar
- ¾ tsp cinnamon
- 2 tbsp tapioca
- 2 tbsp lemon juice
- 1 cup boiling water

DIRECTIONS

1. Toss apples with brown sugar, cinnamon, and tapioca in a medium bowl until evenly coated. Place apples in a Slow Cooker.
2. Pour lemon juice over the top. Pour in boiling water. Cook on high for 3-4 hours.

Nutritions: Calories: 176; Protein: 0 g; Carbohydrates: 46 g; Fat: 0 g; Cholesterol: 0 mg; Fiber: 2 g

185. SWEET POTATO PUDDING

Preparation Time
10 minutes

Cooking Time
50 minutes

Servings
8

INGREDIENTS

- 4 cup cooked and mashed sweet potatoes
- ¾ cup sugar
- ½ cup egg substitute
- ½ cup coconut milk
- 1 tbsp lime juice
- ¼ cup rum
- ½ tsp baking powder
- ½ tsp cinnamon
- ¼ cup raisins

DIRECTIONS

1. Preheat the oven to 350°F (180°C, or gas mark 4). To mashed potatoes, alternate adding sugar and egg substitute, mixing well after each addition.
2. Add coconut milk. Blend well. Mix in lime juice and rum. Mix well. Combine baking powder and cinnamon and add to potato mixture, along with raisins.
3. Mix well. Pour mixture into a greased tube cake or Bundt pan and bake for 50 minutes, or until done.

Nutritions: Calories: 271; Protein: 5 g; Carbohydrates: 53 g; Fat: 4 g; Cholesterol: 0 mg; Fiber: 4 g

186. PUMPKIN COOKIES

Preparation Time: 10 minutes
Cooking Time: 15 minutes
Servings: 30

INGREDIENTS

- 1 tsp baking powder
- 2 cup flour
- ½ tsp baking soda
- 1 tsp cinnamon
- ¼ cup canola oil
- ½ tsp ground ginger
- 6 tbsp egg substitute
- 1 tsp ground allspice
- 1 cup packed brown sugar
- 1 cup canned or cooked fresh pumpkin
- 1 tsp vanilla

DIRECTIONS

1. Preheat the oven to 350°F (180°C, or gas mark 4). Combine flour, baking soda, ginger, cinnamon, baking powder, and allspice in a medium bowl.
2. Beat oil, brown sugar, egg substitute, pumpkin, and vanilla in a wide bowl. Stir flour mixture into wet ingredients until just combined.
3. Drop spoonsful of dough about 1 inch (2.5 cm) apart on an ungreased baking sheet. Bake for 12-14 minutes.

Nutritions: Calories: 81; Protein: 1 g; Carbohydrates: 14 g; Fat: 2 g; Cholesterol: 0 mg; Fiber: 1 g

187. MASCARPONE AND FIG CROSTINI

Preparation Time
10 minutes

Cooking Time
10 minutes

Servings
6-8

INGREDIENTS

- 1 long French baguette
- 4 tbsp (½ stick) salted butter, melted
- 1 (8 oz) tub of mascarpone cheese
- 1 (12 oz) jar of fig jam or preserves

DIRECTIONS

1. Preheat the oven to 350°F. Slice the bread into ¼-inch-thick slices. Layout the sliced bread on a single baking sheet and brush each slice with the melted butter.
2. Put the single baking sheet in the oven and toast the bread for 5-7 minutes, just until golden brown.
3. Let the bread cool slightly. Spread about 1 tsp or so of the mascarpone cheese on each piece of bread. Top with 1 tsp or so of the jam. Serve immediately.

Nutritions: Calories: 445; Fat: 24 g; Carbs: 48 g; Protein: 3 g

188. TRADITIONAL MEDITERRANEAN LOKUM

Preparation Time
25 minutes

Cooking Time
0 minutes

Servings
20

INGREDIENTS

- 1 oz confectioner's sugar
- 3 ½ oz cornstarch
- 20 oz caster sugar
- 4 oz pomegranate juice
- 16 oz cold water
- 3 tbsp gelatin, powdered

DIRECTIONS

1. Line a baking sheet with parchment paper.
2. Mix the confectioner's sugar and 2 oz cornstarch until well combined.
3. In a saucepan, heat the caster sugar, pomegranate juice, and water over low heat.
4. In a mixing bowl, combine 4 oz cold water with the remaining cornstarch. Stir the mixture into the sugar syrup.
5. Slowly and gradually, add in the powdered gelatin and whisk until smooth and uniform.
6. Bring the mixture to a boil, turn the heat to medium and continue to cook for another 18 minutes, whisking constantly, until the mixture has thickened.
7. Scrape the mixture into the baking sheet and allow it to set in your refrigerator.
8. Cut your lokum into cubes and coat them with the confectioner's sugar mixture. Bon appétit!

Nutritions: Calories: 208; Fat: 0.5 g; Carbs: 54.4 g; Protein: 0.2 g

189. MIXED BERRY AND FIG COMPOTE

Preparation Time
20 minutes

Cooking Time
0 minutes

Servings
5

INGREDIENTS

- 2 cup mixed berries
- 1 cup figs, chopped
- 4 tbsp pomegranate juice
- ½ tsp ground cinnamon
- ½ tsp crystallized ginger
- ½ tsp vanilla extract
- 2 tbsp honey

DIRECTIONS

1. Place the fruit, pomegranate juice, ground cinnamon, crystallized ginger, and vanilla extract in a saucepan; bring to medium heat.
2. Turn the heat to a simmer and continue to cook for about 11 minutes, stirring occasionally to combine well. Add in the honey and stir to combine.
3. Remove from the heat and keep in your refrigerator. Bon appétit!

Nutritions: Calories: 150; Fat: 0.5 g; Carbs: 36.4 g; Protein: 1.4 g

190. CREAMED FRUIT SALAD

Preparation Time
10 minutes

Cooking Time
0 minutes

Servings
2

INGREDIENTS

- 1 orange, peeled and sliced
- 2 apples, pitted and diced
- 2 peaches, pitted and diced
- 1 cup seedless grapes
- ¾ cup Greek-style yogurt, well-chilled
- 3 tbsp honey

DIRECTIONS

1. Divide the fruits between dessert bowls.
2. Top with the yogurt. Add a few drizzles of honey to each serving and serve well-chilled.
3. Bon appétit!

Nutritions: Calories: 250; Fat: 0.7 g; Carbs: 60 g; Protein: 6.4 g

191. ALMOND COOKIES

Preparation Time
5 minutes

Cooking Time
10 minutes

Servings
4-6

INGREDIENTS

- ½ cup sugar
- 8 tbsp (1 stick) salted butter, at room temperature
- 1 large egg
- 1 ½ cup all-purpose flour
- 1 cup ground almonds or almond flour

DIRECTIONS

1. Preheat the oven to 375°F. Using a mixer, cream together the sugar and butter. Add the egg and mix until combined.
2. Alternately add the flour and ground almonds, ½ cup at a time, while the mixer is on slow.
3. Once everything is combined, line a baking sheet with parchment paper. Drop a spoonful of dough on the baking sheet, keeping the cookies at least 2 inches apart.
4. Put the single baking sheet in the oven and bake just until the cookies start to turn brown around the edges for about 5-7 minutes.

Nutritions: Calories: 604; Fat: 36 g; Carbs: 63 g; Protein: 11 g

192. CRUNCHY SESAME COOKIES

Preparation Time
10 minutes

Cooking Time
15 minutes

Servings
14-16

INGREDIENTS

- 1 cup sesame seeds, hulled
- 1 cup sugar
- 8 tbsp (1 stick) salted butter, softened
- 2 large eggs
- 1 ¼ cup flour

DIRECTIONS

1. Preheat the oven to 350°F. Toast the sesame seeds on a baking sheet for 3 minutes. Set aside and let cool.
2. Using a mixer, cream together the sugar and butter. Put the eggs one at a time until well-blended. Add the flour and toasted sesame seeds and mix until well-blended.
3. Drop a spoonful of cookie dough onto a baking sheet and form them into round balls, about 1-inch in diameter, similar to a walnut.
4. Put in the oven and bake for 5-7 minutes or until golden brown. Let the cookies cool and enjoy.

Nutritions: Calories: 218; Fat: 12 g; Carbs: 25 g; Protein: 4 g

193. MINI ORANGE TARTS

Preparation Time
45 minutes

Cooking Time
0 minutes

Servings
2

INGREDIENTS

- 1 cup coconut flour
- ½ cup almond flour
- A pinch of grated nutmeg
- A pinch of sea salt
- ¼ tsp ground cloves
- ¼ tsp ground anise
- 1 cup brown sugar
- 6 eggs
- 2 cup heavy cream
- 2 oranges, peeled and sliced

DIRECTIONS

1. Begin by preheating your oven to 350°F.
2. Thoroughly combine the flour with spices. Stir in the sugar, eggs, and heavy cream. Mix again to combine well.
3. Divide the batter into 6 lightly greased ramekins.
4. Top with the oranges and bake in the preheated oven for about 40 minutes until the clafoutis is just set. Bon appétit!

Nutritions: Calories: 398; Fat: 28.5 g; Carbs: 24.9 g; Protein: 11.9 g

194. TRADITIONAL KALO PRAMA

Preparation Time
45 minutes

Cooking Time
0 minutes

Servings
2

INGREDIENTS

- 2 large eggs
- ½ cup Greek yogurt
- ½ cup coconut oil
- ½ cup sugar
- 8 oz semolina
- 1 tsp baking soda
- 2 tbsp walnuts, chopped
- ¼ tsp ground nutmeg
- ¼ tsp ground anise
- ½ tsp ground cinnamon
- 1 cup water
- 1 ½ cup caster sugar
- 1 tsp lemon zest
- 1 tsp lemon juice

DIRECTIONS

1. Thoroughly combine the eggs, yogurt, coconut oil, and sugar. Add in the semolina, baking soda, walnuts, nutmeg, anise, and cinnamon.
2. Let it rest for 1 ½ hour.
3. Bake in the preheated oven at 350°F for approximately 40 minutes or until a tester inserted in the center of the cake comes out dry and clean.
4. Transfer to a wire rack to cool completely before slicing.
5. Meanwhile, bring the water and caster sugar to a full boil; add in the lemon zest and lemon juice, and turn the heat to a simmer; let it simmer for about 8 minutes or until the sauce has thickened slightly.
6. Cut the cake into diamonds and pour the syrup over the top; allow it to soak for about 2 hours. Bon appétit!

Nutritions: Calories: 478; Fat: 22.5 g; Carbs: 62.4 g; Protein: 8.2 g

195. TURKISH-STYLE CHOCOLATE HALVA

Preparation Time: 20 minutes

Cooking Time: 0 minutes

Servings: 2

INGREDIENTS

- ½ cup water
- 2 cup sugar
- 2 cup tahini
- ¼ tsp cardamom
- ¼ tsp cinnamon
- A pinch of sea salt
- 6 oz dark chocolate, broken into chunks

DIRECTIONS

1. Bring the water to a full boil in a small saucepan. Add in the sugar and stir. Let it cook, stirring occasionally, until a candy thermometer registers 250°F. Heat off.
2. Stir in the tahini. Continue to stir with a wooden spoon just until halva comes together in a smooth mass; do not overmix your halva.
3. Add in the cardamom, cinnamon, and salt; stir again to combine well. Now, scrape your halva into a parchment-lined square pan.
4. Microwave the chocolate until melted; pour the melted chocolate over your halva and smooth the top.
5. Let it cool to room temperature; cover tightly with a plastic wrap and place in your refrigerator for at least 2 hours. Bon appétit!

Nutritions: Calories: 388; Fat: 27.5 g; Carbs: 31.6 g; Protein: 7.9 g

196. COOKIES AND CREAM SHAKE

Preparation Time: 15 minutes
Cooking Time: 0 minutes
Servings: 3

INGREDIENTS

- 6 crushed chocolate wafer cookies
- 3 cup fat-free vanilla ice cream
- 1 ⅓ cup chilled vanilla soy milk (soya milk)

DIRECTIONS

1. Combine ice cream and soy milk in a blender. Blend until the mixture is smooth and foamy.
2. Toss in the cookies and pulse a few times to combine.
3. Immediately pour into tall, cold glasses and serve.

Nutritions: Calories: 270; Protein: 9 g; Carbohydrates: 52 g; Fat: 3 g; Cholesterol: Traces; Fiber: 1 g

197. LEMON CHEESECAKE

Preparation Time: 10 minutes
Cooking Time: 20 minutes
Servings: 8

INGREDIENTS

- 1 envelope of unflavored gelatin
- 2 tbsp cold water
- ½ cup skim milk, heat to boiling point
- 2 tbsp lemon juice
- Egg substitute equal to 1 egg or 2 egg whites
- 1 tsp vanilla
- ¼ cup sugar
- Lemon zest
- 2 cup low-fat Cottage cheese

DIRECTIONS

1. Combine the gelatin, water, and lemon juice in a blender container. The process is for 1-2 minutes at low speed to soften gelatin.
2. Add the boiling milk and process until the gelatin is completely dissolved. Add egg replacement, vanilla, sugar, and cheese to a blender container, and blend until smooth.
3. Fill a 9-inch pie pan or a circular flat dish halfway with the mixture. Refrigerate for 2-3 hours. Just before serving, sprinkle with lemon zest if desired.

Nutritions: Calories: 80; Protein: 9 g; Carbohydrates: 9 g; Fat: 1 g; Cholesterol: 3 mg; Fiber: 0.2 g

198. WHOLE-GRAIN MIXED BERRY COFFEECAKE

Preparation Time
10 minutes

Cooking Time
30 minutes

Servings
8

INGREDIENTS

- 1 tbsp vinegar
- ½ cup skim milk
- 1 tsp vanilla
- 2 tbsp canola oil
- ⅓ cup packed brown sugar
- 1 egg
- ½ tsp ground cinnamon
- 1 cup pastry flour, whole-wheat
- ½ tsp baking soda
- ⅛ tsp salt
- ¼ cup low-fat slightly crushed granola
- 1 cup frozen mixed berries, such as raspberries, blueberries, and blackberries
- Cooking spray

DIRECTIONS

1. Preheat the oven to 350°F. Use a cooking spray to coat a cake pan or 8-inch round and coat it with flour.
2. Combine the vinegar, milk, oil, egg, vanilla, and brown sugar in a large mixing bowl and whisk until smooth. Just until moistened, stir in flour, cinnamon, baking soda, and salt. Fold half of the berries into the batter gently. Pour into the pan that has been prepared. Lastly, top with the granola and remaining berries.
3. Bake for 25-30 minutes, or until golden brown and the center of the top snaps back when touched. Cool for 10 minutes in the pan on a cooling rack. Warm the dish before serving.

Nutritions: Calories: 165; Protein: 4 g; Carbohydrates: 26 g; Fat: 5 g; Cholesterol: 24 mg; Fiber: 3 g

199. ALMOND AND APRICOT BISCOTTI

Preparation Time
20 minutes

Cooking Time
60 minutes

Servings
24

INGREDIENTS

- ¼ cup brown sugar, firmly packed
- 2 lightly beaten eggs
- 1 tsp baking powder
- ¾ cup all-purpose flour, plain
- 2 tbsp low-fat 1% milk
- ½ tsp almond extract
- 2 tbsp canola oil
- ¼ cup coarsely chopped almonds
- 2 tbsp dark honey
- ¾ cup whole-wheat flour, whole-meal
- ⅔ cup dried apricots, chopped

DIRECTIONS

1. Preheat the oven to 350°F. Combine the brown sugar, flour, and baking powder in a large mixing bowl. To combine ingredients, whisk them together. Add the milk, eggs, honey, canola oil, and almond extract to a mixing bowl. Stir the dough with a wooden spoon until it barely comes together. Add chopped apricots and almonds. Mix until the dough is well-blended using floured hands.
2. Shape the dough into a flattened log 3 inches wide, 12 inches long, and approximately 1 inch high on a long piece of plastic and wrap it by hand. Transfer the dough to a nonstick baking sheet by lifting the plastic wrap. Bake for 25-30 minutes, or until gently browned. Allow it cool for 10 minutes on another baking sheet.
3. On a cutting board, place the cooled log. Cut 24 ½-inch broad slices diagonally crosswise using a serrated knife. Arrange the slices on the baking sheet, cut-side down. Put it back in the oven and bake for 15-20 minutes, or until crisp. Allow cooling fully before transferring to a wire rack. Keep the container sealed.

Nutritions: Calories: 75; Protein: 2 g; Carbohydrates: 12 g; Fat: 2 g; Cholesterol: 15 mg; Fiber: 1 g

200. APPLE DUMPLINGS

Preparation Time
2 hours

Cooking Time
30 minutes

Servings
8

INGREDIENTS

For the dough:
- 2 tbsp apple liquor or brandy
- 1 tbsp butter
- 2 tbsp buckwheat flour
- 1 tsp honey
- 2 tbsp rolled oats
- 1 cup whole-wheat flour
- Cooking spray

For the apple filling:
- 1 tsp nutmeg
- 6 large thinly sliced tart apples
- Zest of 1 lemon
- 2 tbsp honey

DIRECTIONS

1. Preheat the oven to 350°F. Combine the flour, honey, butter, and oats in a food processor. Pulse a few times more until the mixture resembles a fine meal.
2. Pulse a few more times to incorporate the brandy or apple liquor until the mixture begins to form a ball. Refrigerate it for 2 hours after removing the mixture from the food processor. Combine nutmeg, apples, and honey. Toss in the lemon zest. Set it aside.
3. Extra flour is used to roll out the chilled dough to a thickness of ¼ inch. Using an 8-inch circle cutter, cut the dough into 8-inch circles.
4. Use an 8-cup muffin pan that has been gently sprayed with cooking spray. Place a dough circle over each gently sprayed cup. Gently press dough into place. Fill them with the apple mixture. To seal, fold over the edges, squeeze the top, and bake for 30 minutes or golden brown.

Nutritions: Calories: 178; Protein: 3 g; Carbohydrates: 36 g; Fat: 2.5 g; Cholesterol: 4 mg; Fiber: 1 g

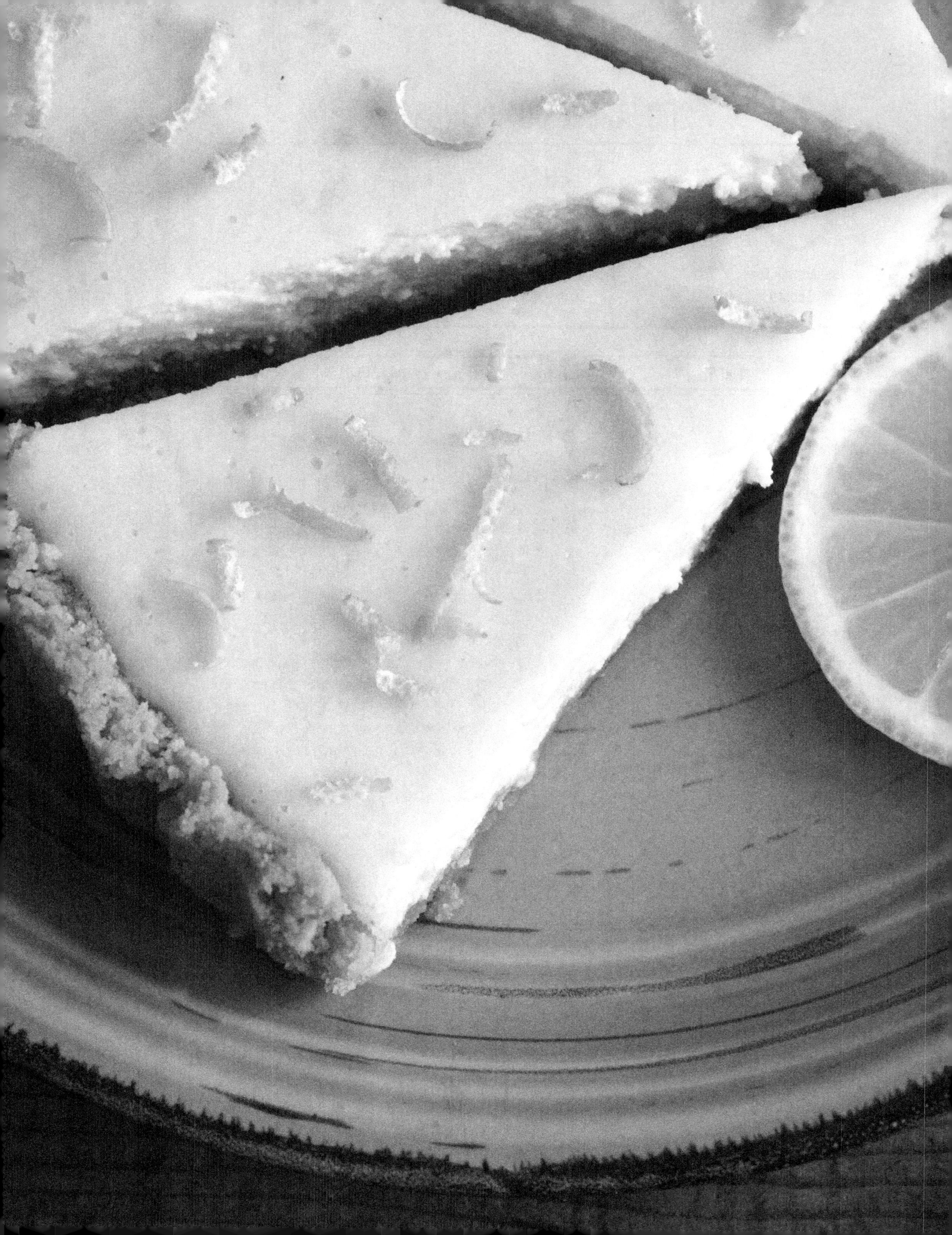

CONCLUSION

The risk of cardiovascular disease increases in proportion to the level of total cholesterol. These conditions include coronary artery disease, a form of heart disease. It is also due to the elevation in LDL cholesterol levels and lower HDL cholesterol levels which are often accompanied by an increased blood sugar level.

Many people have tried to deter their bad cholesterol with diet and exercise, but it is still very high in many cases. Many people believe that there is no benefit from eating plant-based foods when weight loss occurs because the body automatically burns mostly fat for fuel instead of sugar. However, this depends on how efficiently and effectively that person can utilize dietary choices for lowering their bad cholesterol and maintaining a healthy weight.

A scientific study revealed that the optimum diet for lowering cholesterol is a plant-based diet, which is very low in saturated fat and cholesterol. The study group was made of men and women with normal levels of LDL cholesterol, averaging 120 milligrams per deciliter (mg/dL) with an average weight of 200 lb. Over 6 weeks, the subjects were asked to limit animal products and increase plant-based foods to about 50% or more of the total calories.

The results showed that LDL levels fell from an average of 130–107 over 6 weeks. The HDL levels remained constant at an average of 60 mg/dL, however, the LDL levels fell in all of the participants, regardless of age or weight. This excludes the fact that people may have different levels of good cholesterol which are not measured, or what is measured as HDL may actually be bad cholesterol.

The study confirmed that a low-fat diet was beneficial for lowering bad cholesterol. It also showed the ability to reduce LDL and maintain good HDL levels with a plant-based diet. The study group performed extremely well and will probably attribute this outcome to their healthy lifestyle choices.

It is still important to note that drugs have much higher success rates when prescribed than when used as self-prescribed supplements, like statin medication.

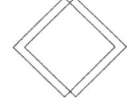

Printed in Great Britain
by Amazon